Inter-State Water Law in the United States of America

International Water Law

Volumes published in this Brill Research Perspectives title are listed at *brill.com/rpwl*

Inter-State Water Law in the United States of America

What Lessons for International Water Law?

By

Rhett Larson

BRILL

LEIDEN | BOSTON

Originally published as Volume 2(3) 2017, in *International Water Law*, DOI 10.1163/23529369-12340007.

Library of Congress Control Number: 2017949010

Typeface for the Latin, Greek, and Cyrillic scripts: "Brill". See and download: brill.com/brill-typeface.

ISBN 978-90-04-35763-1 (paperback)
ISBN 978-90-04-35764-8 (e-book)

This book is printed on acid-free paper and produced in a sustainable manner.

Contents

Inter-State Water Law in the United States of America

What Lessons for International Water Law?

Rhett B. Larson
Richard Morrison Fellow in Water Law, Associate Professor of Law at Arizona State University's Sandra Day O'Connor College of Law, and Senior Research Fellow, Kyl Center for Water Policy, United States
Rhett.larson@asu.edu

Abstract

The rich field of inter-state water law in the United States illustrates both successes and failures in transboundary water management and allocation. This monograph analyzes the three general approaches to water allocation between riparian states to certain shared watercourses in the United States, namely equitable apportionment, congressional apportionment, and inter-state compacts. This analysis is accompanied by a discussion and evaluation of the different cases of shared watercourses that applied these approaches, and a comparison of each of them to similar approaches in international water law. The monograph draws lessons for international water law from inter-state water law—highlighting the successful inter-state approaches that can be adopted by international water law, as well as the approaches that failed, and which should be avoided.

Keywords

Inter-state Water Law – International Water Law – United States of America – Watercourses Convention

Introduction

During recent severe drought conditions in the Western United States, parched states struggled to share the Colorado River.[1] The states that share the Great

---

1 Christine A. Klein, 'Water Bankruptcy,' *Minnesota Law Review*, Vol. 97(2), pp. 560–624 (2012); see also Jesse Reiblich & Christine A. Klein, 'Climate Change and Water Transfers,' *Pepperdine Law Review*, Vol. 41(2), pp. 439–508 (2014).

 | DOI 10.1163/9789004357648_002

Lakes face growing concerns regarding sustainable water use.[2] Southeastern states confront increasing water scarcity in the Chattahoochee River basin.[3] In the dry central plains of the United States, states continue to mine the Ogallala Aquifer.[4] The challenge of sharing water resources across jurisdictional boundaries has been, and continues to be, a source of conflict between states in the United States. But an early 19th Century explorer of the Colorado River basin made an intriguing proposal that could have mitigated, if not avoided, such disputes.

In 1868, the U.S. Congress funded the expeditions of John Wesley Powell into the Colorado River basin and its environs.[5] Thereafter, one of Powell's recommendations to Congress was that Congress should base state boundaries on watersheds of western rivers.[6] Imagine the world as a golf ball—a large sphere covered in divots.[7] Each divot is a drainage basin or catchment, an area of land draining water to a common point.[8] The boundaries separating the catchments are watersheds.[9] Powell argued that basing state boundaries on watersheds would avoid inter-state disputes over shared water resources in the

2 Jonathan Rosenbloom, 'New Day at the Pool: State Preemption, Common Pool Resources, and Non-Place Based Municipal Collaborations,' *Harvard Environmental Law Review*, Vol. 32(2), pp. 445–485 (2012).

3 Joseph W. Dellapenna, 'Inter-state Struggles Over Rivers: The Southeastern States and the Struggle Over the Hooch,' *NYU Environmental Law Journal*, Vol. 12(1), pp. 828–900 (2005); Nathan C. Johnson, 'Protecting Our Water Compacts: The Looming Threat of Unilateral Congressional Interaction,' *Wisconsin Law Review*, Vol. 2010(3), pp. 875–905 (2010).

4 Robert W. Adler, 'Climate Change and the Hegemony of State Water Law,' *Stanford Environmental Law Journal*, Vol. 29(1), pp. 1–61 (2010).

5 See generally John Wesley Powell, *The Exploration of the Colorado River and Its Canyons* (Dover Publications Inc., 1961); John Wesley Powell, *Report on the Lands of the Arid Region of the United States, with a More Detailed Account of the Lands of Utah* (Harvard Common Press, 1983) (1879); William deBuys, ed., *Seeing Things Whole: The Essential John Wesley Powell* (Island Press, 2001); Donald Worster, *A River Running West: The Life of John Wesley Powell* (Oxford University Press, 2001).

6 Wallace Stegner, *Beyond the Hundredth Meridian: John Wesley Powell and the Second Opening of the West* (Penguin Books, 1954), p. 322.

7 Rhett B. Larson, 'Interstitial Federalism,' *UCLA Law Review*, Vol. 62(4), pp. 908–968 (2015), pp. 911–912.

8 Ibid.

9 Craig Anthony Arnold, 'Fourth-Generation Environmental Law: Integrationist and Multimodal,' *William & Mary Environmental Law & Policy Review*, Vol. 35(3), pp. 771–884 (2011), pp. 843–844.

arid west.[10] Congress ignored Powell's recommendation—in some cases, using rivers as state boundaries—and Powell's warning regarding inter-state water disputes has ultimately been vindicated.[11]

In the Colorado River basin, where Powell formulated his recommendations on watershed boundaries, inter-state water disputes nearly resulted in a 20th Century U.S. civil war.[12] The Colorado River basin includes seven states, and the Colorado River forms part of the boundaries between Arizona, California, and Nevada.[13] In 1935, the governor of Arizona, Benjamin Baker Moeur, had spies reporting on California's construction of the Parker Dam on the Colorado River.[14] When his spies alerted him that California construction crews crossed into Arizona territory, Moeur sent the National Guard to halt construction.[15] Harold L. Ickes, the U.S. Secretary of the Interior at the time, intervened to delay dam construction in exchange for Moeur agreeing to recall troops.[16] Only four years before the Parker Dam conflict on the Colorado River, the states of Texas and Oklahoma had a similar dispute over the shared Red River, resulting in Texas ordering rangers to defend bridges and the governor of Oklahoma declaring martial law to secure the state's control over the river.[17] The intensity

---

10 Denial Kemmis, *This Sovereign Land: A New Vision for Governing the West* (Island Press, 2001), p. 177. "I want to present to you what I believe to be ultimately the political system which you have got to adopt in this country, and which the United States will be compelled sooner or later ultimately to recognize. I think each drainage basin in the arid land must ultimately become the practical unit of organization, and it would be wise if you could immediately adopt a county system which would be convenient with drainage basins."

11 Craig Anthony Arnold, 'Adaptive Watershed Planning and Climate Change,' *Environmental & Energy Law & Policy*, Vol. 5(2), pp. 417–487 (2010), p. 420; A. Dan Tarlock, 'The Potential Role of Local Governments in Watershed Management,' *Pace Environmental Law Review*, Vol. 20(1), pp. 149–176 (2002), p. 153.

12 Larson, supra note 7, pp. 912–913.

13 Ibid.

14 Marc Reisner, *Cadillac Desert: The American West and Its Disappearing Water* (Penguin Books, 1993), pp. 256–260.

15 Jon Kyl & Ryan A Smith, 'Foreword: Water Law and Policy Conference,' *Arizona Law Review*, Vol. 49(2), pp. 209–216 (2007), pp. 209–210.

16 A. Dan Tarlock, 'Safeguarding International River Ecosystems in Times of Scarcity,' *University of Denver Water Law Review*, Vol. 3(1), pp. 231–272 (2000); Jack L. August, Jr., *The Vision in the Desert: Carl Hayden and Hydropolitics in the American Southwest* (Texas Christian University Press, 1999), pp. 146–148.

17 Jerry B. Lincecum, 'Red River Bridge War,' *in*, Kenneth L. Untied (ed.), *Folklore in Motion: Texas Travel Lore* pp. 25–34 (University of North Texas Press, 2007), pp. 24–32.

of these inter-state water conflicts in the 1930s led Adolph Hitler to speculate that such disputes were evidence of a growing national disunity that would preclude the United States from entering a global conflict.[18]

While this time in U.S. history reflected a uniquely dramatic period for inter-state water disputes, legal battles between neighboring jurisdictions over shared water sources have featured prominently in inter-state relations from the earliest days of the nation's history.[19] This history can provide lessons of successes to follow and mistakes to avoid in the formulation and implementation of international water law. This monograph uses U.S. inter-state water law to illustrate four legal approaches that may benefit international water management in some instances, and four legal approaches in U.S. inter-state water law that should generally be avoided in international water management. This monograph proceeds in three parts. In Part I, it provides background on inter-state water law in the United States and compares it generally to transboundary water law at the international level.

In Part II, the monograph discusses four approaches of U.S. inter-state water law that may prove helpful in legal disputes under international water law. First, U.S. courts consider principles of water law that two jurisdictions have in common when apportioning water rights between those jurisdictions. Second, the adjudication of inter-state water disputes frequently involves water masters or the oversight of federal agencies with unique water competence and the authority to make efficient and (sometimes) unilateral decisions on water allocations when inter-jurisdictional negotiations fail. Third, inter-state water law in the United States provides certain legal and economic incentives for artificial groundwater recharge and water banking. Fourth, while much of U.S. legal history, including the development of water law, has failed to live up to constitutional aspirations of equality and due process, U.S. water law has laudable aspects that provide strong grounding for the assertion of water rights by indigenous peoples.

In Part III, the monograph argues against four approaches in U.S. water law as mistakes to be avoided in international transboundary water management, including some approaches that have already begun to take root in international water law. First, in many instances, states have different legal regimes

18 Ibid., p. 32; see also Bill Cannon, *Texas: Land of Legend and Lore* 39 (Republic of Texas Press, 2004).

19 See, e.g., *Martin v. Waddell's Lessee*, 41 U.S. 367, 411 (1842); *Pollard's Lessee v. Hagen*, 44 U.S. 212, 216 (1845); *South Carolina v. North Carolina*, 130 S. Ct. 854 (2010); *Montana v. Wyoming*, 131 S.Ct. 1765 (2011).

governing groundwater and surface water, resulting in a bifurcated system that frustrates integrated water resource management and aggravates water disputes. Second, inter-state water law draws arbitrary distinctions between raw water and embedded water that increases legal uncertainty. Third, in some cases, inter-state water rights allocations are based on inaccurate data and incorrect assumptions about the climate and hydrology of the catchment. Fourth, inter-state water law is frequently implemented by inter-state commissions that are either too powerful (resulting in infringement upon the sovereignty of less-powerful member states) or else too weak (resulting in poor water management and enforcement of water regulations). The monograph also proposes reforms in international water law that could avoid such mistakes in transboundary water management.

I Comparing Inter-State and International Water Law

Much of the United States is covered by water bodies that cross state and tribal jurisdictional boundaries, including some of the nation's most significant water sources, like the Great Lakes, Mississippi River, and Ogallala Aquifer.[20] As the legal and non-legal disputes over the Colorado River and Red River in the 1930s illustrates, developing and protecting these shared water resources in the context of inter-jurisdictional politics is a complex governance challenge in the United States, just as transboundary water management presents governance challenges in the international context.[21] These governance challenges

20 Daniel P. Loucks, 'Managing America's Rivers: Who's Doing It?,' *International Journal of River Basin Management*, Vol. 1(1), pp. 21–34 (2003), pp. 21–24. The Ogallala Aquifer is shared between Texas, New Mexico, Oklahoma, Colorado, Kansas, Nebraska, Wyoming, and South Dakota. The Great Lakes are shared between the United States and Canada, but also between the states of Minnesota, Wisconsin, Illinois, Indiana, Michigan, Ohio, Pennsylvania, and New York, as well as the provinces of Quebec and Ontario. The Mississippi River basin is enormous, and includes the states of Louisiana, Mississippi, Arkansas, Oklahoma, Texas, Colorado, Kansas, Missouri, Tennessee, Kentucky, Pennsylvania, Ohio, West Virginia, Indiana, Illinois, Iowa, Nebraska, South Dakota, and Minnesota.

21 Justice Oliver Wendell Holmes, in an inter-state water dispute, noted the role of the federal government in these disputes as essential, because the alternative to federal government intervention is inter-state belligerence and even violence. *Missouri v. Illinois*, 200 U.S. 496, 521 (1906). The Colorado River is shared between Mexico and the United

grow more intransigent as population growth and climate change aggravate water scarcity.[22]

In the United States, there are three general approaches to water rights allocation between states that have corollaries in international water law. Each of the following subsections describes these inter-state water allocation approaches and compares them to approaches in international water law. The first is the doctrine of 'equitable apportionment' developed by the U.S. Supreme Court in cases involving its original jurisdiction over inter-state water disputes.[23] Its international corollary is the principle of reasonable and equitable utilization embodied in Articles 5 and 6 of the United Nations Convention on the Law of Non-Navigational Uses of International Watercourses (the "Watercourse Convention"). The second is 'Congressional apportionment,' whereby U.S. Congress apportions water between states by legislation.[24] The international corollary for Congressional apportionment is a framework treaty like the Watercourse Convention. The third approach to apportioning water rights and managing water shared between co-riparian states is through inter-state compacts. Inter-state compacts are constitutionally-sanctioned agreements between states, enacted into state legislation and approved by Congress.[25] Typically, inter-state water compacts establish commissions comprised of representatives of the member states, and often representatives of federal agencies.[26] The international corollary of the inter-state

---

States, but also between the states of Wyoming, Utah, Colorado, New Mexico, Arizona, Nevada, and California, and the Mexican states of Sonora and Baja California.

22 Noah D. Hall, 'Inter-state Water Compacts and Climate Change Adaptation,' *Environmental & Energy Law & Policy Journal*, Vol. 5(2), pp. 237–323 (2010).

23 U.S. Constitution, art. II, § 2. For a discussion of the principles of equitable apportionment, see *Nebraska v. Wyoming*, 325 U.S. 589 (1945); see also *Colorado v. New Mexico*, 459 U.S. 176 (1982).

24 U.S. Constitution, art. I, § 8, cl. 3; U.S. Constitution art. VI, § 1, cl. 2. For example of Congressional apportionment and its role in resolving inter-state water disputes, see Boulder Canyon Project Act, 45 Stat. 1057 (1928) (codified at 43 U.S.C. § 617–617u (2014)), § 12A [BCPA] and *Arizona v. California*, 373 U.S. 546 (1963); see also Truckee-Carson-Pyramid Lake Water Rights Settlement Act, Pub. L. No. 101–618, 104 Stat. 3294 (1990).

25 U.S. Constitution, art. I, § 10, cl. 3.

26 Robert H. Abrams, 'Water, Climate Change, and the Law: Integrated Eastern States Water Management Founded on a New Cooperative Federalism,' *Environmental Law Reporter, News & Analysis*, Vol. 42(5), pp. 10433–10449 (2012); see also Jeffrey P. Featherstone, 'Existing Interstate Compacts: The Law and the Lessons,' *Toledo Journal of Great Lakes Law, Science, and Policy*, Vol. 4(2), pp. 271–282 (2001), pp. 271–280.

river compact is a basin-level international treaty, with similarly-established basin commissions.

A *Equitable Apportionment and Reasonable and Equitable Utilization*

Some of the earliest U.S. Supreme Court decisions addressed disputes related to inter-state water bodies and the ownership of the beds and banks of navigable rivers.[27] Under the U.S. Constitution, the Supreme Court has original jurisdiction over all inter-state disputes, meaning that when one state sues another state in court, that lawsuit is heard and adjudicated by the Supreme Court with no intervening appeals process.[28] In events John Wesley Powell likely would have foreseen, many of the earliest inter-state disputes in the western United States regarding rivers dealt particularly with boundary disputes where the boundary was the river itself.[29]

These early decisions held that the U.S. federal government holds title to navigable rivers in federal territories in trust for when those territories may be organized into states, thereby ensuring that all states enter the union upon 'equal footing' with the first thirteen states, at least regarding ownership of navigable waters.[30] Navigable waters are those water bodies that were used or were susceptible to being used as highways of commerce at the time of statehood in their ordinary and natural condition.[31] Non-navigable waters could be owned by private parties, while navigable waters are held in trust by the state for the benefit of its citizens.[32] Where navigable waters formed the boundary between states, the boundary was determined to be *ad medium filum aquae*—the 'thread of the stream'—with particular rules impacting those boundaries depending on accretion, avulsion, dereliction, or erosion.[33] These early decisions set a tone favoring state sovereignty over water resources, with a narrow

27 See, e.g., *Martin v. Lessee of Waddell*, 41 U.S. 367 (1842); see also *Shively v. Bowlby*, 152 U.S. 1 (1894).

28 See, e.g., *Louisiana v. Mississippi*, 516 U.S. 221 (1995); *Nebraska v. Wyoming*, 515 U.S. 1115 (1995).

29 A. Dan Tarlock, 'The Law of Equitable Apportionment Revisited, Updated, and Restated,' *University of Colorado Law Review*, Vol. 56(4), pp. 381–411 (1985), pp. 381–384.

30 *PPL Montana, LLC v. Montana*, 132 S. Ct. 1215, 1235 (2012); Eric Biber, 'The Price of Admission: Causes, Effects, and Patterns of Conditions Imposed on States Entering the Union,' *American Journal of Legal History*, Vol. 46(2), pp. 119–208 (2004).

31 *The Daniel Ball*, 77 U.S. 557 (1871).

32 *Lehigh Falls Fishing Club v. Andrejewski*, 123 A.2d 636 (Pa. 1956).

33 *Nebraska v. Iowa*, 143 U.S. 359 (1892).

national role, that would affect how transboundary water disputes were resolved for decades.[34]

These navigability and boundary decisions were essential to the question of inter-state water management in two ways. First, these boundary disputes illustrate how protective individual states frequently are of their sovereignty, particularly sovereignty over water resources within their states or forming a state border.[35] Second, granting title to navigable waters to states under the equal footing doctrine effectively conceded to the states the primary jurisdiction over water apportionment within their boundaries, which created a decentralized, and therefore fairly diverse, amalgam of water rights laws within the United States.[36] States may sue one another under the U.S. Supreme Court's original jurisdiction if a neighboring state violates the sovereignty of another regarding water resources.

In such suits, the U.S. Supreme Court applies the doctrine of equitable apportionment as it has developed over a century.[37] Early equitable apportionment decisions track the preference for state autonomy embodied in the early water boundary dispute cases. In 1907, the U.S. Supreme Court issued its seminal equitable apportionment decision in *Kansas v. Colorado*.[38] In that case, the state of Kansas sought an injunction against Colorado, its neighboring state, in Colorado's use of the transboundary Arkansas River.[39] In rejecting Kansas' petition, the Supreme Court held that the 'diminution of the flow of water in the river by the irrigation of Colorado has worked some detriment to the southwestern part of Kansas, and yet when we compare the amount of this detriment with the great benefit which has obviously resulted in the counties in Colorado, it would seem that equality of right and equity between the two States forbids any interference with the present withdrawal of water in Colorado.'[40] The Court thus established as a major consideration one state's successful economic development relative to Inter-state water apportionment,

34 Robert W. Adler, 'The Ancient Mariner of Constitutional Law: The Historical, Yet Declining Role of Navigability,' *Washington University Law Review*, Vol. 90(2), pp. 1643–1706 (2013).

35 See, e.g., *Nebraska v. Iowa*, 143 U.S. 359 (1892).

36 Josh Patashnik, 'Arizona v. California and the Equitable Apportionment of Inter-state Waterways,' *Arizona Law Review*, Vol. 56(1), pp. 1–51 (2014), p. 41: "The equal-footing doctrine is one of the pillars of American federalism."

37 See, e.g., *Louisiana v. Mississippi*, 516 U.S. 221 (1995); *Nebraska v. Wyoming*, 515 U.S. 1115 (1995).

38 206 U.S. 46 (1907).

39 Ibid.

40 Ibid., pp. 113–114.

at least in the early days of the Court's equitable its co-riparian state in how a court will apportion water between states.

Apportionment decisions thus depended on states effectively out-competing their neighbors economically. If a state wanted more water allocated to it by the U.S. Supreme Court, it needed to show it could make better economic use of that water than its neighbors. However, equitable apportionment developed in the ensuing years to be more nuanced and expansive in the factors the Supreme Court considers in transboundary water allocations. In 1945, in a dispute between the neighboring states of Nebraska and Wyoming, the Supreme Court laid out the factors that it considers in making equitable apportionment determinations.[41] These factors include 'physical and climatic conditions, consumptive use of water in several sections of the river, character and rate of return flows, extent of established uses, availability of storage water, practical effect of wasteful uses on downstream areas, and damage to upstream areas as compared to benefits to downstream areas if a limitation is imposed on the former.'[42]

The Supreme Court's 1945 decision in *Nebraska v. Wyoming* is not only significant for its more nuanced approach to apportionment, but also for its opening the door to greater assertion of national authority of water rights. By supplementing state economic considerations with factors deemed relevant by the federal judiciary, the Supreme Court introduced an embryonic articulation of national water policy aims as a central element in resolving inter-state water disputes.[43] But perhaps more importantly, the U.S. Supreme Court articulated factors for equitable apportionment between states that are strikingly similar to the factors considered for reasonable and equitable utilization determinations under international water law.

The United Nations Convention on the Law of Non-navigational Uses of International Watercourses (the 'Watercourse Convention'), which entered into force on August 17, 2014, sets forth several factors to consider in the reasonable and equitable utilization of water shared between nations.[44] Beyond the obvious use of the word 'equitable' in the articulation of both the inter-state doctrine and the international doctrine, the factors articulated by the U.S. Supreme Court in determining equitable apportionment are similar to

41 *Nebraska v. Wyoming*, supra note 23.

42 Ibid., at 618.

43 Larson, supra note 7, p. 952.

44 Convention on the Law of Non-Navigational Uses of International Watercourses, G.A. Res. 51 Res. 51/229, UN GAOR, 51st Sess., Supp. No. 49, UN Doc. A/RES/51/229 (July 8, 1997) ['UN Watercourses Convention'].

the factors laid out in Article 6 of the Watercourse Convention in determining equitable utilization. The U.S. Supreme Court considers 'physical and climatic conditions,' and international law considers '[g]eographic, hydrographic, hydrological, climatic, ecological and other factors of a natural character.'[45] The U.S. Supreme Court considers consumptive uses, while the Watercourse Convention includes considerations of the 'effects of the use or uses of watercourses.' The U.S. Supreme Court considers wasteful uses, and the Watercourse Convention includes considerations of conservation options.

Despite these similarities, the U.S. doctrine of equitable apportionment and the factors included in determining reasonable and equitable utilization under the Watercourse Convention have differences that are important to note for what each doctrine may learn from the other. The Watercourse Convention expressly includes consideration of population, which seems an obvious factor missing from inter-state water law.[46] Both doctrines, however, may benefit from expressly requiring consideration of projected population growth. The Watercourse Convention considers both existing and potential uses of the watercourse, while the U.S. doctrine of equitable apportionment considers only 'consumptive uses,' not necessarily potential future uses.[47] The Watercourse Convention includes an express consideration of both social and economic needs, while there is no similar consideration of social needs under the U.S. equitable apportionment doctrine.[48] The Watercourse Convention also includes consideration of available alternatives to planned uses in determining equity and reasonableness that the U.S. Supreme Court should also consider in equitable apportionment cases.[49] It might also be helpful for the U.S. doctrine of equitable apportionment to expressly include ecological considerations similar to the Watercourse Convention's considerations, because those considerations may not always be adequately captured by the concept of waste embodied in the U.S. law.[50]

The U.S. equitable apportionment doctrine includes a cost-benefit analysis consideration that could be a helpful factor to evaluate equitable utilization in international water law.[51] Additionally, the consideration of the character

45 Compare the UN Watercourses Convention, ibid., Article 6 with *Nebraska v. Wyoming*, supra note 23, at 618.

46 Ibid.

47 Ibid.

48 Ibid.

49 Ibid.

50 Ibid.

51 Ibid.

and rate of return flows under U.S. inter-state water law may also be a helpful factor to include in determining equitable utilization in international water law.[52] In any event, the similarities of these two doctrines suggest that U.S. inter-state water apportionment law may have influenced how international law evaluates questions of equity in transboundary water allocation, and that the U.S. doctrine of inter-state equitable apportionment and the international doctrine of reasonable and equitable utilization have much to learn from each other.

B *Congressional Apportionment and Framework Treaties*

In some instances, states avoid adjudicating water disputes under the U.S. Supreme Court's original jurisdiction and its equitable apportionment doctrine, and instead allocate water legislatively through the national Congress. The risks of Supreme Court adjudication are obvious, as the number and ambiguity of factors the Supreme Court considers in equitable apportionment makes any prediction of the case outcome difficult. Large, politically-powerful states may prefer to avoid that uncertainty and instead push for national legislation allocating shared water resources. For example, California, one of the largest and most politically-influential states, pushed for Congress to enact the Boulder Canyon Project Act (BCPA) in 1928 to apportion water between the states that share the lower Colorado River basin.[53] The BCPA allocated 4.4 million acre-feet (one acre-foot equals 43,560 m^3) of Colorado River water each year to California, while authorizing California to construct (with federal funds) the Hoover Dam and the All-American Canal to bring irrigation water into agricultural production areas of the state.[54] Despite the BCPA aim to avoid Supreme Court adjudication and to forestall a protracted water dispute between Colorado River basin states, the BCPA precipitated the near-crisis involving National Guard troops and the Parker dam, and ultimately resulted in one of the seminal U.S. Supreme Court decisions in inter-state water law, *Arizona v. California*.[55]

The BCPA was not the last time Congress intervened legislatively in an inter-state water dispute. Congress facilitated and legislative settlement of the water dispute between California, Nevada, and the Lake Paiute Tribe over the Truckee River Basin in the 1990 Truckee-Carson-Pyramid Lake Water Rights

52 Ibid.

53 'BCPA, supra note 24'.

54 Ibid.

55 Supra note 24; see generally Patashnik, supra note 36.

Settlement Act.[56] Contention arose over the shared Truckee basin because heavily-subsidized water was delivered to farms for large-scale irrigation, diminishing water supplies to tribal and urban domestic water uses.[57] State and tribal policies apparently could be not reconciled and arguably failed to adequately account for conflicting uses, leading to tribal and urban stakeholders seeking federal intervention. The success of these stakeholders in securing national legislation can arguably be attributed to their reliance on national environmental protection statutes as a means of circumventing or preempting state water rights regimes.[58]

Congressional apportionment has an arguable international corollary—the development of the framework treaty by a supranational organization like the United Nations. The benefits of such an approach can include a relatively disinterested representative body to arbitrate or supersede otherwise irreconcilable regional laws and norms. On the other hand, such an approach can include too many stakeholders at that high level who are remote from, and thus unfamiliar with, the unique social, economic, ecologic, and hydrologic realities of the basin. Furthermore, one nation with disproportionate influence in the United Nations could impact how framework treaties are formulated and implemented to the detriment of less-influential co-riparian nations. These same drawbacks are seen in pursuing a Congressional apportionment between states in the United States—negotiating with members of the national legislature who do not understand the regional character of the water body in dispute increases transaction costs, and populous and wealthy states exert disproportionate political influence in Congress.

Framework treaties are, of course, different than a Congressional apportionment approach in many ways. Influence in the United Nations is not necessarily the same as influence in the U.S. national legislature, where population and legislative seniority can impact the political power of a state in ways that may not mirror the supranational context. Additionally, the United Nations does not inherently preempt domestic national laws in the same way as national law preempts state law in the United States. Furthermore, the development of framework treaties is sometimes a bottom-up affair.[59] For example, the

---

56 Pub. L. No. 101–618, 104 Stat. 3294 (1990); see also A. Dan Tarlock, 'The Creation of New Risk Sharing Water Entitlement Regimes: The Case of the Truckee-Carson Settlement,' *Ecology Law Quarterly*, Vol. 25(4), pp. 674–691 (1999).

57 Tarlock, ibid., p. 677.

58 Ibid., p. 680.

59 Ryan B. Stoa, 'The United Nations Watercourses Convention on the Dawn of Entry Into Force,' *Vanderbilt Journal of Transnational Law*, Vol. 47(5), pp. 1321–1370 (2014), pp. 1321–1322.

Watercourse Convention is a framework treaty that attempts to embody evolving customary international law by reflecting how regional river treaties are formulated.[60] Congressional apportionment is more frequently a top-down affair, where national legislation is used to overcome regional differences in policy, law, and water use priorities.[61]

Importantly, much of evolving transboundary water law has been built over centuries on the foundation of riparian law inherited by British and Roman colonies that, like the United States, have inter-state water disputes. Australia has a British common law heritage and manages a challenging inter-jurisdictional river, the Murray-Darling, which flows through Queensland, New South Wales, Victoria, and South Australia.[62] As with U.S. inter-state compacts, Australia also established the Murray-Darling Commission to allocate rights between states, and recognized vested, saleable water rights which are constrained by commission management authority, similar to the common law concept of riparian rights subject to reasonableness determinations.[63] The commission was created by national legislation and wields significant control, and thus reflects many of the benefits and challenges associated with U.S. Congressional apportionment.

India also has a British common law heritage and a federal system where water rights are largely governed by states, with some watercourses flowing across state boundaries.[64] As with Congressional apportionment in the U.S., much of inter-state water disputes in India are governed by national legislation—the Interstate Water Dispute Act of 1956.[65] Unlike Congressional apportionment, however, the national legislation in India does not necessarily allocate water between jurisdictions, but instead provides a mechanism to petition the national government for an impartial adjudication involving transboundary water rights.[66] In a sense, that approach is a hybrid of equitable apportionment by the U.S. Supreme Court and Congressional apportionment. But such claims under the Interstate Water Dispute Act may also result in inter-jurisdictional negotiations resulting in agreements on water sharing similar to inter-state compacts in the United States. India thus finds a way to

60 A. Dan Tarlock, 'Towards a More Robust International Water Law of Cooperation to Address Droughts and Ecosystem Conservation,' *Georgetown Environmental Law Review*, Vol. 28(2), pp. 261–290 (2016), p. 271.

61 Larson, supra note 7, p. 959.

62 Tarlock, supra note 16, pp. 263–264.

63 Ibid.

64 Salman Salman, 'Inter-States Water Disputes in India: An Analysis of the Settlement Process,' *Water Policy*, Vol. 4(3), pp. 223–237 (2002).

65 Ibid.

66 Ibid.

integrate the two approaches to inter-state water dispute resolution already discussed—national legislative apportionment and equitable apportionment by courts—with the final approach relied on in inter-state water disputes in the United States, inter-jurisdictional agreements regarding water rights, or inter-state compacts.

C *Inter-State Compacts and Regional Treaties*

The two approaches to inter-state water rights allocations—and their international corollaries—discussed above share certain limitations. Evaluations under equitable apportionment, and its reasonable and equitable utilization international counterpart, include consideration of factors that are highly nuanced and yet also ambiguous in meaning. This nuance and ambiguity make the outcome of such evaluations unpredictable. These factors tend to be highly technical and require a knowledge of and sensitivity toward unique regional conditions. The adjudicative body evaluating these factors must therefore have the requisite institutional competency to effectively integrate and evaluate these factors.

Congressional apportionment and its framework treaty counterpart have related limitations. In this case, water policy for a basin is not evaluated, but instead formulated, by a legislative body that may be unfamiliar with unique regional conditions. If a governance institution is smaller than the catchment, the jurisdictions can generate negative externalities on their neighbors, by damming or polluting a river, for example.[67] These negative externalities were quite possibly what drove John Wesley Powell's concerns regarding using rivers as state boundaries.

If we draw the jurisdictional boundary more broadly—to encompass multiple catchments—then policy formulation and implementation involves too many remote stakeholders unfamiliar with the unique regional conditions of the water body.[68] Essentially, in drawing jurisdictional boundaries for water management, narrow, intra-basin jurisdictions create negative externalities

67 Robert L. Glicksman & Richard E. Levy, 'A Collective Action Perspective on Ceiling Preemption by Federal Environmental Regulation: The Case of Global Climate Change,' *Northwestern University Law Review*, Vol. 102(2), pp. 579–648 (2008), pp. 579–94; Ronald Coase, 'The Problem of Social Cost,' *Journal of Law & Economics*, Vol. 3(1), pp. 1–44 (1960), pp. 1–14.

68 Marco Schäferhoff et al., 'Transnational Public-Private Partnerships in International Relations: Making Sense of Concepts, Research Frameworks, and Results,' *International Studies Review*, Vol. 11(3), pp. 451–474 (2009).

and broad, multi-basin jurisdictions create high transaction costs.[69] In either event, efficient water policy formulation and implementation may be stifled.

To avoid these pitfalls, the jurisdictional boundaries of water governance institutions should correspond to the watershed, with basin-level governance internalizing costs while retaining institutional competency and low transaction costs.[70] Under the 'internalization prescription for government jurisdiction,' power should be assigned over public goods like water 'to the smallest unit of government that internalizes the effects of its exercise.'[71] Where jurisdiction is already drawn either too broadly or too narrowly, inter-jurisdictional agreements can approximate the ideal basin-scale jurisdiction.

In the U.S. context, the U.S. Supreme Court recognized the limitations of overly-broad or overly-narrow jurisdiction over transboundary waters. In another water dispute between the states of Colorado and Kansas, the Supreme Court noted that inter-state water adjudications 'involve the interests of quasi-sovereigns, present complicated and delicate questions, and, due to the possibility of future change of conditions, necessitate expert administration rather than judicial imposition of a hard and fast rule.'[72] Among the Supreme Court's chief concerns were state sovereignty and states' ability to address unique and changing regional conditions.

In the case of equitable apportionment, a national entity is applying national law to an inter-state problem, but concerned with state sovereignty and local conditions. The Court, recognizing this inherent tension, went on to write that '[s]uch controversies may appropriately be composed by negotiation and agreement, pursuant to the compact clause of the federal Constitution. We say of this case, as the court has said of inter-state differences of like nature, that such mutual accommodation and agreement should, if possible, be the medium of settlement instead of invocation of our adjudicatory power.'[73] Effectively, the Supreme Court is calling for redrawing jurisdictional boundaries to correspond to the watershed to avoid negative externalities, lower transaction costs,

---

69 Larson, supra note 7, p. 909.

70 A watershed is the boundary between catchments or basins. A catchment, or basin, is the area providing runoff and stream flow to a mainstream and tributaries. See generally J. A. Stanford & J. V. Ward, 'Management of Aquatic Resources in Large Catchments: Recognizing Interactions between Ecosystem Connectivity and Environmental Disturbance,' *in*, Robert J. Naiman (ed.), *Watershed Management: Balancing Sustainability and Environmental Change*, pp. 91–124 (Springer, 2002), pp. 91–93.

71 Robert D. Cooter, *The Strategic Constitution* (Princeton University Press, 2000), p. 107.

72 *Colorado v. Kansas*, 320 U.S. 383, 392 (1943); see also *Nebraska v. Wyoming*, supra note 23, at 616.

73 Ibid., at 392–393.

and harness the expertise of local stakeholders through inter-jurisdictional agreements.[74]

Such a redrawing of jurisdictional boundaries in the United States necessitates the negotiation of an inter-state compact—an agreement between states approved by the national Congress—which then creates and empowers an inter-state commission to govern the transboundary water.[75] Inter-state compacts are usually negotiated by governors and other state officials, and typically include involvement from relevant federal legislators and agencies. Once effective, these agreements have the force and supremacy of national law.[76] Inter-state compacts typically establish a governing commission to oversee and implement the terms of the compact—with varying degrees of funding, enforcement authority, and adjudicative or permitting powers.[77]

Inter-state water governance has not evolved in a linear way from equitable apportionment by the Supreme Court, to Congressional apportionment, to the implementation of inter-state compacts and commissions. The history of governing the Colorado River provides an example of how each of these approaches can overlap with one another. The BCPA constituted an attempt at Congressional apportionment, the Supreme Court's decision in *Arizona v. California* included evaluations of equitable apportionment, and the states sharing the Colorado River ultimately agreed to the Colorado River Basin Compact and created the Colorado River Commission in 1928.[78] Each of these legal approaches remains relevant in the inter-state management of the Colorado River. Indeed, the complex transboundary management of the Colorado River features many positive and negative lessons for inter-jurisdictional water law, which is discussed in more detail below.

---

74 Erin Ryan, 'Negotiating Federalism,' *Boston College Law Review*, Vol. 52(1), pp. 1–136 (2011), pp. 4–12.

75 Article I, section 10 of the U.S. Constitution provides that 'No State shall, without the Consent of Congress ... enter into any Agreement or Compact with another State, or a foreign Power. See also *Texas v. New Mexico*, 482 U.S. 124, 128 (1987) and Noah Hall & Benjamin Cavataro, 'Inter-state Groundwater Law in the Snake Valley: Equitable Apportionment and a New Model for Transboundary Aquifer Management,' *Utah Law Review*, Vol. 2013(3), pp. 1553–1626 (2013), pp. 1553–1572.

76 See *Culyer v. Adams*, 449 U.S. 433, 438 (1981); see also Jill Elaine Hasday, 'Inter-state Compacts in a Democratic Society: The Problem of Permanency,' *Florida Law Review*, Vol. 49(1), pp. 1–47 (1997), pp. 1–14.

77 Robin Kundis Craig, 'Constitutional Contours for the Design and Implementation of Multistate Renewable Energy Programs and Projects,' *University of Colorado Law Review*, Vol. 81(3), pp. 771–832 (2010), p. 826.

78 Colorado River Compact, 70 Cong. Rec. 325 (1928); *Arizona v. California*, supra note 24.

Most inter-state river basins in the United States are not directly governed by an inter-state compact, but inter-state river compacts nevertheless remain an important national water governance tool. There are currently 37inter-state river basin compacts that, when taken together, govern the vast majority of both the land mass and population of the country.[79] In almost every instance, the inter-state compact creates an inter-state river basin commission, though as already noted, the actual authority held by these commissions can vary significantly from basin to basin.[80] As the product of negotiation of an inter-state agreement, state-level legislation, and national Congressional approval, inter-state river basin compacts and their related commissions do not fit comfortably into any binary conception of national and local administration.[81]

Inter-state compacts and commissions governing inter-state waters in the United States are similar in many respects to the kinds of regional transboundary treaties that govern many international water bodies around the world.

79 Inter-state Water Apportionment Compacts: Alabama-Coosa-Tallapoosa River Basin Compact, Animas-La Plata Project Compact, Apalachicola-Chattahoochee-Flint River Basin Compact, Arkansas River Basin Compact, Bear River Compact, Belle Fourche River Compact, Big Blue River Compact, Bi-State Metropolitan Development District Compact, California-Nevada Inter-state Compact, Canadian River Compact, Colorado River Compact, Connecticut River Compact, Costilla Creek Compact, Delaware River Basin Compact, Great Lakes Basin Compact, Klamath River Compact, La Plata River Compact, New England Inter-state Water Pollution Control Compact, New Hampshire-Vermont Inter-state Sewage and Waste Disposal Facilities Compact, Ohio River Valley Water Sanitation Compact, Potomac Valley Compact, Pecos River Compact, Red River Compact, Red River of the North Compact, Republican River Compact, Rio Grande Inter-state Compact, Sabine River Compact, Snake River Compact, South Platte River Compact, Susquehanna River Basin Compact, Tennessee River Basin Water Pollution Control Compact, Thames River Flood Control Compact, Tri-State Sanitation Compact, Upper Colorado River Basin Compact, Upper Niobrara River Compact, Wheeling Creek Watershed Protection & Flood Prevention Compact, Yellowstone River Compact. Seven were created by federal statute (Bear River, Delaware River, Great Lakes, Potomac, New England, Ohio, and Susquehanna). See http://www.fws.gov/laws/lawsdigest/compact.html.

80 See generally Interstate Council on Water Policy, 'Inter-state River Basin Organization Source Water Protection Survey' *Interstate Council on Water Policy* (February 2012), http://www.icwp.org/cms/ic/Inter-stateReport_new.pdf (last accessed April 11, 2017). River basin commissions vary in size and resources, with staffs ranging from one to 45, and annual budgets ranging from US$20,000 to more than US$16 million

81 See, e.g., Blake Hudson, 'Reconstituting Land-Use Federalism to Address Transitory and Perpetual Disasters: The Bimodal Federalism Framework,' *BYU Law Review*, Vol. 2011(6), pp. 1991–2061 (2011); Ernest A. Young, 'The Rehnquist Court's Two Federalisms,' *Texas Law Review*, Vol. 83(1), pp. 1–165 (2004).

Regional treaties govern critical water bodies all over the world.[82] As with inter-state compacts, such treaties require negotiation between two jurisdictions, often including approval of national legislatures, and the involvement of supranational bodies as well, whether as arbiters, adjudicators, facilitators, advisors, or financiers.[83] And as with inter-state commissions, these treaties frequently attempt to approximate the idea of the internalization prescription by establishing basin-level multinational commissions. The goals animating these regional approaches are arguably the internalization of costs associated with water management, the integration of management with regional and local expertise, and the minimization of transaction costs associated with water resource development and protection.[84]

But this approach inevitably gives rise to difficulties in both the inter-state and international context. How do the contracting jurisdictions maximize the potential benefits of the bargain without sacrificing sovereignty? What is the appropriate geographic scope of the inter-jurisdictional entity—the entire basin, a sub-basin, or a stream segment? Should inter-basin issues such as desalination, cloud-seeding, and forestry management increase the geographic scope, and if so, does that defeat the very purpose of inter-jurisdictional, basin-level governance? How do less populous/powerful/wealthy jurisdictions create and retain leverage in negotiating the inter-jurisdictional management of shared resources? Nearly two centuries of inter-state river basin commissions in the United Stats have attempted to answer these difficult questions while still operating under both U.S. Supreme Court and national Congressional authorities. Some attempts to answer these questions in the U.S. inter-state context have generated innovations and successes that could benefit international transboundary management if appropriately adapted and implemented.

---

82 See, e.g., The 2002 Charter of Waters of the Senegal River, 2002, http://iea.uoregon.edu/pages/view_treaty.php?t=2002-SenegalRiverWaterCharter.EN.txt&par=view_treaty_html [http://perma.cc/6C3R-4KWU] (archived September 21, 2014); Treaty Between the United States of America and Mexico Respecting the Utilization of the Colorado and Tijuana Rivers and of the Rio Grande, United States-Mexico, February 3, 1944, 59 Stat. 1219 [1944 Rivers Treaty]; Acordo sobre o Aquífero Guarani [Agreement on the Guarani Aquifer], August 2, 2010, Argentina-Brazil-Paraguay-Uruguay, Ministério Das Relações Exteriores [Brazilian Ministry of Foreign Affairs] [Acordo].

83 For an overview of general principles impacting international water treaties, see generally Laurence Boisson de Chazournes, *International Law and Freshwater: The Multiple Challenges* (Edward Elgar, 2013).

84 For a discussion of the aims of international water law, see Edith Brown Weiss, 'The Coming Water Crisis: A Common Concern of Humankind,' 1(1) *Transnational Environmental Law*, Vol. 1(1), pp. 153–168 (2012).

II Positive Inter-State Lessons for International Water Law

Part II discusses what innovations and successes the United States has achieved in transboundary water management, and how those might be adapted into the international context. In particular, this Part describes four different aspects of inter-state water law and policy in the United States that have proven relatively successful and which might be adapted for implementation at the international level: (1) the consideration of legal principles held in common between jurisdictions sharing water resources; (2) the reliance on water masters to facilitate water rights negotiations; (3) the establishments of incentives for artificial groundwater recharge; and (4) the recognition of water rights held by indigenous peoples.

A *Considering Commonly-held Water Law Principles*

As discussed above, when U.S. states sue one another over transboundary water apportionment, the U.S. Supreme Court adjudicates those claims based on equitable apportionment factors. The Supreme Court clearly expressed those factors in its decision in *Nebraska v. Wyoming*, a list of factors mirroring many of the considerations of reasonable and equitable utilization under the Watercourse Convention.[85] However, the *Nebraska v. Wyoming* decision was not the first equitable apportionment decision, and prior decisions include additional considerations that are not included in the Watercourse Convention and which might better inform the evaluation of reasonable and equitable utilization under international water law.

For example, in 1907 the U.S. Supreme Court considered the growing population and expanding economy of the state of Colorado, as compared to Kansas' shrinking economy and population, in allocating water between the two states.[86] As such, the U.S. Supreme Court considers projected population and economic growth in apportioning transboundary waters between states. The factors used to evaluate reasonable and equitable utilization of water in international law under the Watercourse Convention do consider existing population, but not necessarily projected population growth.[87] Furthermore, while Article 6 of the Watercourse Convention is forward-looking in the sense that it factors in 'potential uses' of the watercourse, it does not necessarily consider projected economic growth in the different jurisdictions.[88] A more explicitly

85 *Nebraska v. Wyoming*, supra note 23.

86 *Kansas v. Colorado*, 206 U.S. 46, 113–114 (1907).

87 UN Watercourses Convention, supra note 44, art. 6(1)(c).

88 Ibid., art. 6(1)(e).

forward-looking approach to reasonable and equitable utilization, modeled after the considerations the U.S. Supreme Court used in *Kansas v. Colorado*, may prove important—though not dispositive—factors in apportioning international water rights.

Another early equitable apportionment case before the U.S. Supreme Court established perhaps an even more important factor that could be incorporated into international reasonable and equitable utilization analysis. In the United States, states are typically considered the trustee of water, granting their citizens usufructory water rights based on one of two water rights regimes, one applied largely in the eastern states and the other largely in western states.[89] The approach to water rights in eastern states is generally common law riparian rights based on British and Roman laws, under which rights are apportioned to owners of property abutting water bodies based on the requirement that uses be reasonable use.[90]

The approach to water rights in western states is generally prior appropriation, with water rights based on a first-in-time, first-in-right scheme, subject to beneficial use requirements and the prohibition against waste.[91] This approach was driven by public policies to encourage settlements in arid regions of the country in the 19th Century by promising the earliest settlers rights to limited water resources.[92] Neighboring U.S. states sharing transboundary waters can therefore have dramatically different approaches to allocating water rights and different policy aims in water management. These differences have aggravated inter-state water disputes between states over transboundary waters.

The U.S. Supreme Court, in one of its earliest equitable apportionment decisions in 1911, established a critical factor in inter-state water allocation law. The Supreme Court's decision in *Bean v. Morris*, written by Justice Oliver Wendell Holmes, applied state law—in particular, the doctrine of prior appropriation—to decide an inter-state water dispute.[93] In *Bean*, Holmes'

89 Richard M. Frank, 'The Public Trust Doctrine: Assessing its Recent Past and Charting its Future,' *UC Davis Law Review*, Vol. 45(3), pp. 665–691 (2012), pp. 665–677.

90 Shelley Ross Saxer, 'The Fluid Nature of Property Rights in Water,' *Duke Environmental Law & Policy Forum*, Vol. 21(1), pp. 49–112 (2010).

91 Robin Kundis Craig, 'A Comparative Guide to Western States' Public Trust Doctrines: Public Values, Private Rights, and the Evolution Toward an Ecological Public Trust,' *Ecology Law Quarterly*, Vol. 37(1), pp. 53–197 (2010); Joseph W. Dellapenna, 'The Evolution of Riparianism in the United States,' *Marquette Law Review*, Vol. 95(2), pp. 53–90 (2011), pp. 53–65.

92 Keith Hirokawa, 'Some Pragmatic Observations about Radical Critique in Environmental Law,' *Stanford Environmental Law Journal*, Vol. 21(1), pp. 225–235 (2002).

93 221 U.S. 485, 496–487 (1911).

rationale for using state law in an inter-state water dispute was that both states involved in the dispute—Montana and Wyoming—relied on prior appropriation laws, and thus could not fairly deny priority based on prior appropriation when both were bound by similar 'first-in-time, first-in-right' law.[94] The Supreme Court solidified the *Bean* approach of applying state law to inter-state disputes when states shared common water rights laws in *Wyoming v. Colorado*.[95] In that case, the Court again applied prior appropriation principles to decide a transboundary water dispute between two prior appropriation jurisdictions.[96]

A transboundary approach that values shared legal principles can be problematic, as broader, supra-jurisdictional interests are not necessarily consistent with the interests of the jurisdictions sharing the watercourse. Inter-state water disputes cannot always be easily resolved by the U.S. Supreme Court applying what the Court perceives to be shared legal principles between the states.[97] Even jurisdictions sharing water rights principles (like prior appropriation) can have dramatically different policy aims, as well as ecologic and economic concerns.[98] A straight-forward application of shared water law principles, as in *Bean*, became increasingly difficult as state water rights law became ever more differentiated, complicated, and adapted to specific unique conditions.[99] Furthermore, a focus on commonalities in state water rights regimes could exclude consideration of the water rights held by Native American tribes in the shared watercourse.[100]

The focus on shared water law principles across boundaries began to be integrated with other factors in determining equitable apportionment of inter-state watercourses. For example, the role of state law was ultimately downgraded from controlling in cases like *Bean* and *Wyoming* to a 'guiding principle'

94 Robert Glennon & Jacob Kavkewitz, '"A Smashing Victory?" Was *Arizona v. California* a Victory for the State of Arizona?,' *Arizona Journal of Environmental Law & Policy*, Vol. 4(1), pp. 1–38 (2013), pp. 2–17.

95 259 U.S. 419 (1922).

96 Ibid., at 455; see also Glennon & Kavkewitz, supra note 94, p. 24.

97 See Dellapenna (2005), supra note 3, pp. 828–830 (stating that resolving issues in the Apalachicola-Chattahoochee-Flint River Basin was difficult because 'the Florida and Georgia governments had such diametrically opposed agendas for the river.').

98 See Craig, supra note 91.

99 See, e.g., Gregory J. Hobbs, Jr., 'Eighth Update to Colorado Water Law: An Historical Overview,' *University of Denver Water Law Review*, Vol. 16(1), 137 (2012).

100 See generally *Winters v. United States*, 207 U.S. 564 (1908) [*Winters*]; see also Seth Davis, 'Tribal Rights of Action,' *Columbia Human Rights Law Review*, Vol. 45(2), pp. 499–551 (2014).

in the Supreme Court's decision in *Nebraska v. Wyoming*.[101] International water law could similarly look to using domestic water law principles held in common between two nations sharing a watercourse as a factor in the evaluation of reasonable and equitable utilization. Two nations are likely to view such a factor as reasonable and equitable if based on domestic laws already accepted and legitimized under domestic law.

The shared legal heritage of many regions creates commonalities in water rights regimes shared across national borders. For example, much of the water law in the Middle East and North Africa still retains legal principles carried over from the Ottoman Civil Code, the Majalla.[102] Pragmatic and political concerns have resulted in these principles yielding to some degree to more recent legal models and a diversified water rights approach in the region. However, the idea that water is communal property, with prioritization for human and animal consumption, remains a Majalla principle shared across much of the former Ottoman Empire.[103] Furthermore, important legal principles surrounding the contract law codified in the Majalla remain shared across Jordan, Iraq, Syria, and Saudi Arabia, and may be relevant to understanding and interpreting water treaty rights, as well as contracts associated with the development, transport, treatment, and sale of water.[104]

Similarly, former Roman and British colonies have retained elements of riparian rights whose roots lay in those two empires.[105] The core of the riparian rights doctrine is the requirement that all uses of the watercourse be reasonable.[106] The scope of influence of this particular water rights regime is such that it forms not only a common underpinning of many nation's domestic water rights regimes, but also of international water law, including the reasonable and equitable utilization concept embodied in the Watercourse

---

101 Supra note 23; see also Glennon and Kavkewitz, supra note 94, p. 25.

102 Thomas Naff, 'Islamic Law and the Politics of Water,' *in*, Joseph W. Dellapenna & Joyeeta Gupta (eds.), *The Evolution of the Law and Politics of Water*, pp. 37–52 (Springer, 2008).

103 Ibid.; see also Thomas Naff & Joseph Dellapenna, 'Can There be a Confluence? A Comparative Consideration of Western and Islamic Fresh Water Law,' *Water Policy*, Vol. 4(6), pp. 465–489 (2002).

104 P. Nicholas Kourides, 'The Influence of Islamic Law on Contemporary Middle Eastern Legal Systems: The Formation and Binding Force of Contracts,' *Columbia Journal of Transnational Law*, Vol. 9(1), pp. 384–435 (1970), p. 385.

105 Ludwik A. Teclaff, 'Evolution of the River Basin Concept in National and International Water Law,' *Natural Resources Journal*, Vol. 36(2), pp. 359–391 (1996).

106 A. Dan Tarlock, *Law of Water Rights and Resource* (Thomson Reuters, 2000), para. 3:12.

Convention.[107] Riparian rights' reasonable doctrine, and its roots in two imperial legal systems, distinguished between 'artificial uses' of water and 'natural uses.'[108] Under riparian rights regimes, competing water uses are evaluated based on their relative 'reasonableness.'[109] Different jurisdictions apply different standards and consider different factors in making this evaluation.[110] However, many systems with roots in British and Roman riparian rights regimes distinguish between natural uses and artificial uses.[111] Natural uses are typically *per se* reasonable, whereas artificial uses are subjected to an evaluation of their reasonableness relative to competing uses.[112] Natural uses are those required for basic human subsistence at the household level—sufficient for farming, livestock watering, drinking, sanitation, and hygiene.[113] Any use beyond this household-level subsistence is deemed artificial, and subject to a reasonableness evaluation in comparison to other uses in the watercourse.[114]

This distinction, because of its roots in British and Roman law, could be a helpful way of evaluating the meaning of Article 10(2) of the Watercourse Convention, which requires that reasonable and equitable utilization evaluations should give 'special regard ... to the requirements of vital human needs.' The widely-shared riparian principles of reasonableness between domestic water laws grounded in imperial codes may provide guidance on how to give such 'special regard'—perhaps by drawing the same distinction between natural and artificial uses. Where two countries share domestic water law based on riparian principles, international law should rely on that shared principle as guidance in determining allocations and use prioritization. Such allocations and priorities should favor natural uses (ensuring access to a minimum quantity of water for subsistence farming, stock watering, and household-level sanitation, hygiene, and drinking water) in a way similar to the prioritization given under national riparian water rights regimes. Of course, many co-riparian

107 Margaret J. Vick, 'The Law of International Waters: Reasonable Utilization,' *Chicago-Kent Journal of International & Comparative Law*, Vol. 12(1), pp. 141–178 (2012).

108 Eugene F. Ware, *Roman Water Law: Translated from the Pendects of Justinian* (West Publishing, 1905), p. 34; Joshua Getzler, *A History of Water Rights at Common Law* (Oxford University Press, 2004), p. 25.

109 Vick, supra note 105, p. 4.

110 Chad A. West, 'For Body, Soul, or Wealth: The Distinction, Evolution, and Policy Implications of a Water Ethic,' *Stanford Environmental Law Journal*, Vol. 26(1), pp. 201–234 (2007), pp. 201–220.

111 See David H. Getches, *Water Law in a Nutshell* 4th ed. (West Academic, 2009), pp. 34–40.

112 Ibid.

113 Ibid.

114 Ibid.

nations have very little in common between their domestic water laws and policies, and even where they do, those commonalities should be treated as guiding principles—as they are between states in the U.S.—and not determinative. Commonly shared water law principles would serve as another consideration among many in determining reasonable and equitable utilization in international water law.

B *Reliance on Water Masters to Facilitate Negotiation*

The complexities of adjudicating or determining transboundary water allocations require uniquely technical and varied competencies. Typically, in equitable apportionment cases in the U.S. Supreme court, the Court appoints a 'special master' to oversee the adjudication of inter-state water rights.[115] The special master plays a critical role in inter-state water disputes in the U.S., including taking evidence, summoning witnesses, issuing subpoenas, fixing times and conditions of filing, directing proceedings, making factual findings, and providing recommendations to the U.S. Supreme Court regarding motions and rulings.[116]

The special master plays several important roles in promoting an efficient adjudication of transboundary disputes. First, the special master generally has greater specialized competency in the highly technical and interdisciplinary field of water law in comparison to the more generalist court overseeing the adjudication.[117] Second, the special master can expedite the process by functioning as a full-time factfinder to the resolution of a dispute upon which frequently hangs the water supply of millions of people.[118] Delays in such cases can have serious costs, and special masters can make such adjudications more efficient.[119] Third, the power of a special master to unilaterally impose requirements and restrictions on transboundary water regimes can be seen as the sword of Damocles hanging over a dispute, compelling the parties to reach a mutually-agreeable resolution lest the special master's power to allocate by fiat fall on all parties indiscriminately. The U.S. Supreme Court is typically highly

---

115 Dellapenna (2005), supra note 3, p. 883.

116 Anne-Marie C. Carstens, 'Lurking in the Shadows of Judicial Process: Special Masters in the Court's Original Jurisdiction Cases,' *Minnesota Law Review*, Vol. 86(2), pp. 625–715 (2002), pp. 625–655; L. Elizabeth Sarine, 'The Supreme Court's Problematic Deference to Special Masters in Inter-state Water Disputes,' *Ecology Law Quarterly*, Vol. 39(2), pp. 535–569 (2012), pp. 535–551.

117 Carstens, ibid., p. 683.

118 Ibid., p. 641.

119 Ibid., p. 696.

deferential to the fact-finding reports and legal recommendations made by its special master in transboundary water dispute cases.[120]

This third role has obvious drawbacks. The special master can effectively usurp an otherwise relatively transparent adjudicative process or a participatory negotiation and impose the will of a single person who lacks the legitimacy of a democratic election or even appointment by one who was democratically elected.[121] However, that very threat is what encourages jurisdictions potentially subject to the risk of the caprice of the special master to pursue cooperative management of the transboundary waterbody.

The inter-state management of the Colorado River may illustrate how this seemingly negative aspect of the role of the special master's singular power can lead to positive results in inter-jurisdictional cooperation. Most states sharing the Colorado River basin agreed to the Colorado River Compact in 1922.[122] The Compact divides the river roughly equally between the upper basin states (areas residing above Lee's Ferry in Arizona, including a small portion of northern Arizona, Utah, Wyoming, Colorado, and New Mexico) and the lower basin states (most of Arizona, California, and Nevada).[123] The upper and lower basins each receive 7.5 million acre feet per year.[124]

Arizona did not sign the Colorado River Compact until 1944, after it had a commitment from the national government to finance the Central Arizona Project (CAP)—a canal system to divert Arizona's allocation of the river from its western border to use in central Arizona, where most of the state's population resides.[125] Thereafter, California promoted a legislative solution in the BCPA, which vested authority in the U.S. Secretary of the Interior to divide the lower basin allocation with 4.4 million acre-feet to California, 2.8 million acre-feet

120 Ibid.

121 See generally Carstens, supra note 116 (providing a catalogue of critiques over the role and power of the special master in U.S. Supreme Court original jurisdiction cases).

122 Colorado River Compact, supra note 78.

123 Douglas L. Grant, 'Inter-state Water Allocation Compacts: When the Virtue of Permanence Becomes the Vice of Inflexibility,' *University of Colorado Law Review*, Vol. 74(4), pp. 105–180 (2003), pp. 105–116.

124 Ibid.; see also Boulder Canyon Project Act of 1928, Pub. L. No. 642, 45 Stat. 1057, 1060, 1064 (1928) (partially codified, as amended, at 43 U.S.C. §§ 617–617(t) (1994)); *Arizona v. California*, supra note 24, at 564–584.

125 Lawrence J. MacDonnell, '*Arizona v. California*: Its Meaning and Significance for the Colorado River and Beyond After Fifty Years,' *Arizona Journal of Environmental Law & Policy*, Vol. 4(1), pp. 88–129 (2013), pp. 88–95.

to Arizona, and 0.3 million acre-feet to Nevada per year.[126] The U.S. Supreme Court's decision in *Arizona v. California* effectively implemented these allocations and affirmed the broad authority of the Secretary of the Interior to unilaterally alter those allocations in times of shortage.[127] In connection with securing funding for the CAP, Arizona also agreed to be the junior priority user in the lower basin (meaning Arizona would take the initial loss of water from any shortage declaration by the Secretary of the Interior, while California would face no reduction in times of drought).[128]

Following years of failed negotiations between the lower basin states on how to respond to shortages in the river, the U.S. Secretary of the Interior instituted shortage sharing guidelines in 2007.[129] Under these guidelines, the Secretary of the Interior declares a shortage based on the elevation of Lake Mead, the largest reservoir for the lower basin states on the Colorado River.[130] If Lake Mead falls below 1,075 feet on January 1 of any year, a light shortage is declared and Arizona loses 320,000 acre-feet and Nevada loses 13,000 acre-feet.[131] If the level falls below 1,050 feet, a heavy shortage is declared and Arizona loses 400,000 acre-feet and Nevada loses 17,000.[132] If the level falls below 1,025 feet, an extreme shortage is declared and Arizona loses 480,000 acre-feet and Nevada loses 20,000 acre-feet.[133] California would not lose any Colorado River water under any of these shortage declarations.[134]

Recent and ongoing developments in the basin may impact how lower basin jurisdictions cooperate over shortages. For example, Mexico temporarily

---

126 Eric L. Garner & Michelle Ouellette, 'Future Shock? The Law of the Colorado River in the Twenty-First Century,' *Arizona State Law Journal*, Vol. 27(3), pp. 469–506 (1995), pp. 469–473.

127 *Arizona v. California*, supra note 24, at 564–584.

128 Karl Kohlhoff & David Roberts, 'Beyond the Colorado River: Is an International Water Augmentation Consortium in Arizona's Future?,' *Arizona Law Review*, Vol. 49(2), pp. 257–286 (2007), pp. 257–279.

129 Bureau of Reclamation, Colorado River Interim Guidelines for the Operation of Lower Basin Shortages and Coordinated Operations for Lake Powell and Lake Mead, 73 FR 19873–01 (2008); see also James H. Davenport, 'Softening the Divides: The Seven Colorado River Basin States' Recommendation to the Secretary of the Interior Regarding Lower Basin Shortage Guidelines and the Operation of Lakes Mead and Powell in the Low Reservoir Conditions,' *University of Denver Water Law Review*, Vol. 10(2), pp. 287–312 (2007).

130 Ibid.

131 Ibid.

132 Ibid.

133 Ibid.

134 Ibid.

agreed to accept less than the 1.5 million acre-feet of Colorado River water owed to it under the 1944 Rivers Treaty in shortage declarations and to store some of its allocations in U.S. reservoirs under Minute 319 to avoid shortage declarations.[135] Additionally, the lower basin states are in continuing talks regarding shortage sharing and conservation to address drought conditions, including the potential that California will accept sharing in shortage as part of a Drought Contingency Plan (DCP).[136]

The risk of having the Secretary of the Interior make unilateral determinations regarding how jurisdictions share in shortage on the river is arguably one of the drivers of the ongoing DCP negotiations. A similar approach, with similar risks, could be employed to encourage cooperation in transboundary international river basins in other parts of the world. For example, river basin treaties could implement adaptive regimes, with allocations made as a percentage of stream flow, with that percentage based on the types of considerations embodied in Article 6 of the Watercourse Convention regarding reasonable and equitable utilization. Under the treaty, the stream flow percentage allocations would be revisited by the signatory nations for review and possible revision on a regular basis. If states cannot agree to an allocation within a specified time period, the treaty could designate a three-person panel, whose membership would be agreed upon by treaty states at the time of the signing, who could then serve a similar function to that of the special master or Secretary of the Interior. The risk of having allocation choices taken from them would encourage cooperation between co-riparian nations, and the agreement on panel membership would address the concerns of legitimacy that might otherwise plague allocation choices made by special masters in the United States. Furthermore, reliance on a three-person panel might avoid the risks of arbitrariness and disproportionate influence from political interests outside of the basin that may exist in the role the Secretary of the Interior plays in shortage determinations in the Colorado River basin. Such an approach may be fraught

---

135 See 1944 Rivers Treaty, supra note 82; see also Intnternationall Boundary and Water Commission [IBWC], Minute 319: Interim International Cooperative Measures in the Colorado River Basin through 2017 and Extension of Minute 318 Cooperative Measures to Address the Continued Effects of the April 2010 Earthquake in the Mexicali Valley, Baja California (November 20, 2012) [IBWC Minute 319]; Jonathan S. King, Peter W. Culp, & Carlos de la Parra, 'Getting to the Right Side of the River: Lessons for Binational Cooperation on the Road to Minute 319,' *University of Denver Water Law Review*, Vol. 18(1), pp. 35–114 (2014), pp. 36–93.

136 John Fleck, 'On the Brink of a Major Deal to Reduce Colorado River Water Use,' *Inkstain* (November 6, 2016), available at http://www.inkstain.net/fleck/2016/11/brink-major-deal-reduce-colorado-river-water-use/.

enough that nations would not agree *ex ante* in a treaty to risk relinquishing sovereignty to such a process, but that very risk may be critical to spur cooperation in the management of international watercourses.

One possible corollary of the special master or the Secretary of the Interior in the U.S. context is the fact finding commission of the Watercourse Convention.[137] The Watercourse Convention provides that a 'Fact-finding Commission shall be established, composed of one member nominated by each party concerned and in addition a member not having the nationality of any of the parties concerned chosen by the nominated members who shall serve as Chairman.'[138] This fact-finding commission is intended to facilitate equitable and expeditious dispute resolution procedures between co-riparian nations.[139] Regional treaties can further empower a fact-finding commission established and governed under rules similar to those set forth in Article 33 of the Watercourse Convention with authority to impose unilaterally water allocations based on reasonable and equitable utilization principles if the parties fail to reach an agreement on their own. This procedural sword of Damocles would hang over inter-riparian nation negotiations in a way similar to the Secretary of the Interior or special master decisions facilitate negotiations between states in the United States.

C *Incentives for Artificial Groundwater Recharge*

The inter-state issues that face the Colorado River states in the United States provide another example of a potential legal reform for international watercourse management. Lower basin states have successfully used artificial groundwater recharge with surface water taken from the transboundary Colorado River to enhance flexibility in water management through the Arizona Water Banking Authority (AWBA) in the Colorado River basin.[140] Arizona created the AWBA in 1996 as a means of storing Arizona's allocation of Colorado River water in years when it did not use the entire allocated amount.[141] Arizona's geology allows it to artificially recharge depleted aquifers with its Colorado River water, effectively

137 UN Watercourses Convention, supra note 44, art. 33(4).

138 Ibid.

139 Stephen C. McCaffrey, 'The International Law Commission Adopts Draft Articles on International Watercourses,' *American Journal of International Law*, Vol. 89(2), pp. 395–404 (1995).

140 Dean Waters Price, 'The Legal and Historical Barriers to Out-of-District Transfers from Mainstream Colorado River Irrigation Districts in Arizona,' *University of Denver Water Law Review*, Vol. 15(1), pp. 5–29 (2011).

141 Kyl & Smith, supra note 15 , pp. 209–213.

storing Colorado River water for future use as groundwater.[142] Arizona has expanded the AWBA from storing only Arizona's allocation of Colorado River water to contracting with California and Nevada to store allocations on their behalf.[143] In this way, Arizona takes economic advantage of its geologic conditions that make storage possible, and monetizes its own water efficiency by storing and selling unused allocations on behalf of co-riparian nations, who pay Arizona for the storage service.[144]

Arizona relies on the Colorado River as well to recharge depleted aquifers in central Arizona. The CAP includes the Central Arizona Groundwater Replenishment District (CAGRD), which takes a portion of the state's Colorado River allocation for artificial groundwater recharge.[145] Generally speaking, land in central Arizona cannot be subdivided and developed without demonstrating consistency with a goal of safe yield in groundwater management by 2025—meaning that for every drop of groundwater withdrawn to support that developed land, another drop must recharge the aquifer by the year 2025.[146] Most developments in central Arizona are members of the CAGRD, which uses Colorado River water to help those developments achieve the safe yield goal established by the Arizona Groundwater Management Act.[147] CAGRD recharge sites are selected based on their suitability for recharge.

The use of surface water in groundwater recharge in the Colorado River basin illustrates the concept of 'shared benefits' of water development and a potential model for some international watercourses. The 1961 Columbia River Treaty is an example of the concept of 'shared benefits' at work in international water law.[148] The concept of 'shared benefits' is derived from welfare economics, noting that water is a valuable, scarce commodity with multiple possible alternative uses, and the most effective use is often dictated by geography.[149]

---

142 Ibid.

143 Ibid.

144 Ibid.

145 Arizona Revised Statutes §§ 48–3771 to –3783.

146 Arizona Revised Statutes §§ 48–3771–3772(A).

147 Ibid.

148 Treaty Between Canada and the United States of American Relating to Cooperative Development of the Water Resources of the Columbia River Basin, January 17, 1961, 542 *UNTS* 244 (1964).

149 A. Dan Tarlock & Patricia Wouters, 'Are Shared Benefits of International Waters an Equitable Apportionment?' *Colorado Journal of International Environmental Law & Policy*, Vol. 18(1), pp. 523–536 (2007), pp. 523–533; Claudia W. Sadoff & David Grey, 'Beyond the River: The Benefits of Cooperation on International Rivers,' *Water Policy*, Vol. 4(5), pp. 389–403 (2002).

The Columbia River Treaty requires co-riparian nations—the United States and Canada—to make geographically-suitable and economically efficient use of their respective allocations, and then share the benefits of that use with its co-riparian.[150]

In this treaty, Canada agreed to forego certain water development projects within the basin for irrigation in uplands with limited arable soil, and instead develop hydroelectric and flood control facilities to benefit the downstream U.S. users who are better suited for food production.[151] This is perhaps the quintessential example of shared benefits in an international river basin. The upstream jurisdiction is a rocky, mountainous region, well-suited for hydroelectric energy production and flood control, but ill-suited for irrigation. The downstream riparian is a lowland area with slow-moving streams and fertile soil, ideally suited for food production. Each jurisdiction could attempt to capture the full panoply of water uses, but that would mean inefficient attempts to implement uses that may be a poor geographic or economic fit.[152] Instead, the jurisdictions engage in benefit sharing by developing water based on their comparative advantages and equitably sharing benefits across the basin.

Groundwater recharge is another possible avenue for benefit sharing at the international level. Riparian nations with the appropriate hydrogeology could use water from the shared watercourse for artificial groundwater recharge. That nation could store water on behalf of itself and its co-riparians, who could pay the storing nation for that service. In times of shortage, the storing nation could agree to forego a portion of its allocation from the shared watercourse and rely instead on storage groundwater, when appropriate. Such benefit sharing is not only more efficient and geographically-tailored, but has the potential to improve overall cooperation and enhance the adaptive capacity of the transboundary water management regime.[153] As such, a jurisdiction with geological storage capacity through artificial recharge should share the benefits of that storage while accepting other benefits in exchange, including infrastructure financing, energy sales, or food. This type of shared benefits could apply equally to sub-national or indigenous community groups with the appropriate geological conditions for groundwater recharge.[154]

150 Tarlock & Wouters, ibid.

151 Ibid.

152 See generally Rachael Paschal Osborn, 'Climate Change and the Columbia River Treaty,' *Washington Journal of Environmental Law & Policy*, Vol. 2(1), pp. 75–124 (2012).

153 Larson, supra note 7.

154 Ibid.

If the AWBA is capable of banking on behalf of co-riparian states, a logical extension might include banking on behalf of Mexico as well. Mexico could agree to bank any excess water with the AWBA, and then have Arizona release a portion of its Colorado River water allocation to Mexico in drought years, with Arizona withdrawing water banked in its aquifers. Under Minute 319, Mexico agreed to store a portion of its Colorado River allocation in Lake Mead in Arizona.[155] A similar agreement could be reached regarding storage in Arizona aquifers.

Benefit sharing need not be limited solely to water allocations or drought resilience, as is the case with groundwater recharge mechanisms or the Columbia River Treaty. For example, a nation that remediates a contaminated transboundary water or aquifer to increase the water body's assimilative capacity could be compensated by co-riparians for that improved water quality, either directly or based on a cap-and-trade system whereby credits could be sold to those discharging to the stream or aquifer. Water credits could be awarded to the remediating nation and available for purchase by permitted dischargers to the water body as a means of improving and maintaining water quality while providing economic incentives for remediation.[156] Shared benefits may thus not only be a path for integrating groundwater recharge considerations into transboundary water management, but also surface and groundwater quality considerations.

D *Recognition of Indigenous Peoples' Water Rights*

Indigenous groups in the United States could engage in such benefit sharing projects because U.S. law recognizes vested property rights in water held by Native American communities.[157] In the western United States, Native American tribes hold significant claims to water rights. The majority of the 56 million acres of Native American tribal land is located within those states as well.[158] When the U.S. government reserves federal public land for any reason, including reservations for Native American tribes, it implicitly reserves water rights.[159] These rights are called *Winters* rights after the Supreme Court

155 IBWC Minute 319, supra note 135.

156 Rhett B. Larson, 'Innovation and International Commons: The Case of Desalination under International Law,' *Utah Law Review*, Vol. 2012(2), pp. 759–819 (2012).

157 Ibid.

158 Lubowski, Ruben, Marlow Vesterby, Shawn Bucholtz, Alba Baez, and Michael J. Roberts, *Major Uses of Land in the United States, 2002*, EIB-14 (U.S. Department of Agriculture, Economic Research Service, 2006), p. 35.

159 *Arizona v. California*, supra note 24, at 601; *Winters*, supra note 100.

case *Winters v. United States*,[160] which established the doctrine of implicitly-reserved tribal water rights. The amount of water reserved to the tribe is the minimum amount of water necessary to meet the primary purpose of the reservation.[161] The 'primary purpose' of Indian reservations is to establish a permanent homeland.[162] To quantify the amount of water necessary to achieve this purpose, courts have generally used the Indian reservation's practicably irrigable acreage or PIA.[163] However, courts in Arizona engage in a reservation-specific approach to quantifying tribal rights by considering factors like tribal culture, current and projected population, and water use plans.[164] In prior appropriation regimes like Arizona and California, the priority date for tribal *Winters* rights is time immemorial, thus establishing strong legal protection for indigenous water rights, even if not always recognized as such by courts and legislatures.[165]

While far from perfect, the recognition of *Winters* rights held by tribes has allowed tribes to effectively intervene in transboundary water disputes between states in the Supreme Court and facilitate binding settlements and national legislation ensuring tribal access to transboundary water sources.[166] Additionally, while the PIA approach to quantification has obvious limitations and is somewhat antiquated in its insistence on basing quantification on an assumption of agricultural uses, the approach taken in Arizona demonstrates how a more nuanced and adaptive approach can be implemented within the *Winters* rights regime.

A similar approach to recognizing the rights of indigenous communities to water resources could improve the integration of socio-political, cultural, and ecological concerns of these communities in the management of international watercourses. And while a broad, comparative examination of domestic water law is outside the scope of this paper, it is important to note that the United States is only one of many nations that recognize the water rights of

160 *Winters*, ibid.

161 *Cappaert v. United States*, 426 U.S. 128, 141 (1976); see also *United States v. New Mexico*, 438 U.S. 696, 718 (1978).

162 *Winters*, supra note 100, at 576–577.

163 *Arizona v. California*, supra note 24, at 595–601. Included in calculating the PIA is total acreage, arability of the land, and engineering and economic feasibility. *In re* Gen. Adjudication of All Rights to Use Water in Big Horn River System, 753 P.2d 76, 101 (Wyo. 1988), *aff'd*, *Wyoming v. United States*, 492 U.S. 406 (1989).

164 *In re* the Gen. Adjudication of All Rights to Use Water in the Gila River System & Source, 35 P.3d 68, 78–80 (Ariz. 2001).

165 *United States v. Adair*, 723 F.2d 1394, 1414 (9th Cir. 1983).

166 *Arizona v. California*, supra note 24, at 590.

indigenous peoples to some degree. For example, in Ecuador, the Ecuadorian Constitution recognizes the rights of indigenous communities to 'participate in the use, usufruct, administration, and conservation of natural renewable resources' associated with their ancestral lands.'[167] This right has been integrated into and deployed as a means of enhancing tribal political leverage and control over natural resources through water 'juntas,' which are water use districts or cooperatives formed uniquely by indigenous groups in Ecuador to finance and develop water infrastructure.[168] Other Andean countries have similar approaches regarding indigenous water juntas.[169] In cases such as these, the recognition of commonly-held domestic water law principles involving the rights of indigenous peoples by international water commissions could facilitate improved participation and cooperation with tribal groups.

Even where co-riparian nations do not have shared legal principles regarding indigenous water rights, international law may nevertheless provide some leverage to indigenous groups seeking recognition of water rights to be able to access and influence transboundary water management decisions.[170] In 1948, the Organization of American States General Assembly adopted Article 39 of its Charter of Social Guaranties, requiring member states to take 'necessary measures' to protect the property of indigenous peoples.[171] In 1992, the United Nations Conference on Environment and Development in Rio de Janeiro recognized Agenda 21, which included the full participation of water-user groups and indigenous peoples in water management decision-making.[172] Article 25 of the United Nations Declaration on the Rights of Indigenous Peoples provides that indigenous peoples 'have the right to maintain and strengthen their

---

167 Constitution of Ecuador, arti. 57(6) (2008).

168 See generally Rutgerd Boelens, Armando Guevara-Gil, & Aldo Panfichi, 'Indigenous Water Rights in the Andes: Struggles Over Resources and Legitimacy,' *Journal of Water Law*, Vol. 20(5), pp. 268–277 (2009).

169 Ibid.

170 David H. Getches, 'Indigenous Peoples' Rights to Water Under International Norms,' *Colorado Journal of International Environmental Law & Policy*, Vol. 16(1), pp. 259–294 (2005).

171 Inter-American Charter of Social Guarantees, 1948, art. 39, reprinted *in*, Edmund Jan Osmańczyk (ed.), *Encyclopedia of the United Nations and International Agreements*, pp. 763, 1012 (Taylor & Francis, 2003) 012.

172 United Nations Conference on Environment and Development, Agenda 21, UN Doc. A/CONF.151/26 (Vol. II) (1992).

distinctive spiritual relationship with their traditionally owned or otherwise occupied and used land, territories, [and] waters.'[173]

The enforceability and binding status of such international statements and principles can be debated and will vary between nations based on their status as signatories, persistent objectors, and the extent to which such principles have achieved the status of binding customary international law.[174] They may nevertheless in some instances, and perhaps more so in the future, form the basis of a *Winters*-like approach to indigenous water rights recognition and quantification, and ultimately to greater participation and influence from indigenous groups in the formulation and implementation of international water law.

Notably, the international agreements and declarations noted above frequently make reference to socio-cultural considerations associated with indigenous communities' water rights. Transboundary water management regimes can approximate the kind of recognition of indigenous water rights in the United States by more effectively integrating such socio-cultural considerations into management decisions through a more inclusive and collaborative framework.[175] Stakeholders in such transboundary management regimes—including in particular riparian nations and indigenous communities sharing transboundary rivers—will be unlikely to invest in a collaborative manner in a basin-level governance institution like a treaty-established basin commission if they view such a commission as indifferent or hostile to their interests.[176] Indigenous communities should be part of a basin commission that promotes inclusive and transparent stakeholder participation.[177] The aim of such a process should be to integrate indigenous interests into management decisions, as

---

173 United Nations Declaration on the Rights of Indigenous Peoples, G.A. Res. 61/295, UN Doc. A/RES61/295 (September 13, 2007), p. 10.

174 Rhett B. Larson, 'Holy Water and Human Rights: Indigenous Peoples' Religious-Rights Claims to Water Resources,' *Arizona Journal of Environmental Law & Policy*, Vol. 2(1), pp. 81–109 (2011), pp. 81–91.

175 Rachel A. Kitze, 'Moving Past Preemption: Enhancing the Power of Local Governments Over Hydraulic Fracturing,' *Minnesota Law Review*, Vol. 98(1), pp. 385–418 (2013), pp. 385–413 (noting that one of the main weaknesses of even strong interstitial federalism institutions is 'the lack of formal and meaningful involvement of local government representatives in these commissions.').

176 Erin Ryan, supra note 74. p. 130; see also Matthew J. Parlow, 'Civic Republicanism, Public Choice Theory, and Neighborhood Councils: A New Model for Civic Engagement,' *University of Colorado Law Review*, Vol. 79(3), pp. 137–188 (2008).

177 Jeffrey T. Matson, 'Inter-state Water Compact Version 3.0: Missouri River Basin Compact Drafters Should Consider an Inter-Sovereign Approach to Accommodate Federal and Tribal Interests in Water Resources,' *North Dakota Law Review*, Vol. 88(1), pp. 97–138 (2012).

well as to facilitate an equitable allocation of rights and benefits in the shared watercourse to those communities. Tribes could have appointed representatives to basin-level commissions and even be signatories to treaties governing transboundary waters on tribal lands, and participate in the mediation and resolution of transboundary water disputes.

Tribes are only one group that has often been marginalized or excluded from participation in transboundary water management. Other non-state actors, such as non-governmental organizations dedicated to environmental protection and sustainability, natural resource development companies, and public utilities, may also not be included in transboundary water governance institutions like basin commissions. The legitimacy of such institutions, and their ability to secure sufficient funds and maintain sufficient oversight and enforcement power, may be enhanced by the participation of such stakeholders.[178] While greater participation of non-state actors may enhance legitimacy and improve funding, too much participation from non-state stakeholders may unnecessarily increase transactions costs, and too much influence from non-state stakeholders can threaten the perceived legitimacy of these institutions, because those non-state stakeholders are not elected or appointed by democratically-elected officials.[179]

The concerns and values of these non-state stakeholders may be effectively integrated into transboundary water governance institutions without unnecessarily increasing transaction costs or threatening the commission's legitimacy. This may be achieved through a 'new governance' approach involving a decentralized, representative group of stakeholders encouraged to engage in self-regulation in exchange for contributing expertise and providing stakeholder input.[180] In this type of new governance model, transboundary water governance institutions may orchestrate 'regulatory standard-setting,' or the

---

178 See, e.g., Robert F. Weber, 'New Governance, Financial Regulation, and Challenges to Legitimacy: The Example of Internal Models Approach to Capital Adequacy Regulation,' *Administrative Law Review*, Vol. 62(3), pp. 783–869 (2010), pp. 783–844; Melvin Woodhouse, 'Is Public Participation a Rule of the Law of International Watercourses?,' *Natural Resources Journal*, Vol. 43(1), pp. 137–183 (2003), pp. 137–139.

179 See generally Michael J. Gilligan, 'The Transaction Costs Approach to International Institutions, Power, Interdependence and Non-State Actors,' *in*, Helen V. Milner & Andrew Moravcsik, eds., *Power, Interdependence and Nontstate Actors in World Politics*, pp. 50–65 (Princeton University Press, 2009); for an example of how inclusion of non-state actors in natural resource management decisions can threaten the legitimacy of institutions, see *National Park & Conservation Association v. Stanton*, 54 F. Supp. 2d 7 (D.D.C. 1999).

180 Kenneth W. Abbott & Duncan Snidal, 'Strengthening International Regulation Through Transnational New Governance: Overcoming the Orchestration Deficit,' *Vanderbilt Journal of Transnational Law*, Vol. 42(1), pp. 501–578 (2009), pp. 501–510.

cooperative promulgation by non-state actors of voluntary, nonbinding standards of conduct and data-sharing.[181] Where non-state stakeholders cooperate to voluntarily assume such standards and obligations, transboundary basin commissions could provide expedited permitting processes, or decreased penalties for violations disclosed through voluntary audit and reporting protocols. This collaborative 'new governance' approach facilitates the integration of the unique expertise and socio-cultural values of non-state actors into water management decisions through incentives for voluntary engagement.

Still, more reforms may be required to more effectively integrate indigenous communities in the governance of transboundary waters. One potential foundation upon which to build greater recognition of the rights of indigenous communities to water resources is Article 20 of the Berlin Rules, prepared by the International Law Association (ILA) in 2004.[182] The Berlin Rules are not binding international law, *per se*, but the ILA represents a large scholarly non-governmental organization whose membership includes many leading international law experts and aims to codify evolving international law and represent customary international law.[183] Under Article 20 of the Berlin Rules, riparian nations 'shall take all appropriate steps to protect the rights, interests, and special needs of communities and of indigenous peoples or other particularly vulnerable groups likely to be affected by the management of waters, even while developing the waters for the benefit of the entire State or group of States.'[184] One possible appropriate step is for an international river basin commission, including stakeholder participation from the indigenous communities, to quantify the rights of indigenous communities in a manner similar to that of the courts in the state of Arizona, under which communities would have a quantified percentage of the stream flow of transboundary waters with the quantity based on factors like culture, current and projected population, and water use plans.

181 Ibid., p. 507; see also Robert H. Abrams, 'Transboundary Water Allocation Risks of Compacts: Who Wins When Legal Rules Face Adaptive Challenges,' *Rocky Mountain Mineral Law Institute*, Vol. 60, c. 9–1 (2014).

182 International Law Association, 'Final Report of the Water Resources Law Committee, in Report of the Seventy-First Conference of the International Law Association,' *International Law Association* (2004), http://www.ila-hq.org/pdf/Water%20Resources/Final%20Report%202004.pdf [Berlin Rules].

183 Salman Salman, 'The Helsinki Rules, the UN Watercourses Convention and the Berlin Rules: Perspectives on International Law,' *Water Resources Development*, Vol. 23(4), pp. 625–640 (2007).

184 Berlin Rules, supra note 182, p. art. 20.

III Negative Inter-State Lessons for International Water Law

Despite the promise of the innovations in the transboundary inter-state water law in the United States discussed above, such inter-state water law has at least as many lessons regarding pitfalls to avoid in transboundary water management. This section evaluates four mistakes in inter-state water law that should be avoided in the development and implementation of international water law: (1) the bifurcation of groundwater and surface water rights; (2) the arbitrary distinction between surface water, groundwater, and virtual water in regulating commerce; (3) the failure to base water rights allocations on sound data; and (4) the inappropriate empowerment of river basin commissions.

A *Problem of Bifurcated Water Rights Regimes*

One of the most vexing mistakes that the United States has made, and many of its states have made, is bifurcating its surface water rights regime from its groundwater rights regime. Arizona, for example, has a bifurcated water rights system, wherein surface water operates under one set of legal rules (largely prior appropriation, as discussed above), and groundwater operates under an entirely different set of rules (with some areas having water rights based on a prescribed quantity or pumping capacity, or others based on a reasonableness requirement).[185] This legal distinction between surface water and groundwater is critical in states with bifurcated systems, because it determines not only what rules apply to a water right, but also whether or not a right is subject to the certain rights adjudications or the priority system of surface water regimes.[186] However, there is no simple way to draw a hydrologic line between surface water and groundwater.[187]

A shallow well drilled near a river may be pumping mostly water from the river itself, despite all the water being subsurface. In Arizona, water that is underground, but more closely associated with the surface water body is called 'subflow' and is subject to surface water rights law.[188] A deeper well located

185 Abbot & Snidal, supra note 180, pp. 501–510.

186 For an overview of the importance and complexity of the subflow question, see generally Robert Glennon & Thomas Maddock, III, 'In Search of Subflow: Arizona's Futile Effort to Separate Groundwater from Surface Water,' *Arizona Law Review*, Vol. 36(2), pp. 567–607 (1994).

187 Ibid.

188 Allison Evans, 'The Groundwater/Surface Water Dilemma in Arizona: A Look Back and a Look Ahead Toward Conjunctive Management Reform,' *Phoenix Law Review*, Vol. 3(1), pp. 269–292 (2010) (discussing the challenges associated with Arizona's bifurcated water rights system).

further from the river may be pumping mostly water from an aquifer in the phreatic zone, but could nevertheless still be taking some water more closely associated with the surface. Even a well drilled below an aquitard may have a cone of depression that extends to a point that it still draws water that directly impacts stream flow. It is unclear in such instances which water rights regime should be applied. This uncertainty is one of the major factors preventing resolution of decades-long water rights adjudications in Arizona.[189]

But the United States has also made a similar mistake with regards to transboundary water allocations between states. There is currently no inter-state compact established for the transboundary management of groundwater, and many of the nation's inter-state river compacts do not expressly integrate surface water and groundwater. Transboundary water law in the U.S. is ill-equipped to draw a defensible line between the managed surface water and the unmanaged groundwater. This has led to a largely bifurcated approach to inter-state water law in the United States, as illustrated by a recent U.S. Supreme Court case involving transboundary water management.

In the case of *Nebraska v. Kansas* in 2015, the two states that share a river appealed to the U.S. Supreme Court in their dispute over its inter-state allocation.[190] The dispute involved Nebraska pumping water from wells that were hydraulically connected to the Republican River. The two states had agreed to an allocation of the river under the Republican River Compact in 1942.[191] However, that agreement did not address any pumping from wells that might impact stream flow. Kansas complained that Nebraska was violating the inter-state compact, and Nebraska countered that the wells were not subject to an agreement that addressed only the allocation of the river. The two states reached a settlement under which Nebraska agreed to limit pumping its wells in exchange for certain concessions regarding the Platte River. However, Kansas later claimed that Nebraska violated this settlement agreement and brought suit in the U.S. Supreme Court. Had the original inter-state compact integrated both surface water and groundwater in its allocation, the dispute might have been avoided, or at the very least, the U.S. Supreme Court would have had a mutually-agreed upon allocation of all transboundary waters upon which to adjudicate the dispute.

International water law appears to be heading down the precarious path to bifurcated systems that is frustrating transboundary management of the waters

189 See generally Rhett Larson & Kelly Kennedy, 'Bankrupt Rivers,' *UC Davis Law Review*, Vol. 49(4), pp. 1335–1383 (2016).

190 *Kansas v. Nebraska*, 135 S. Ct. 1042 (2015).

191 Ibid.; see also Republican River Compact, Kan. Stat. Ann. §82a–518 (1942).

shared by Kansas and Nebraska. International groundwater law is itself a nascent field. The Guarani Aquifer Treaty, between Brazil, Argentina, Paraguay, and Uruguay, represents the first international groundwater treaty.[192] Jordan and Saudi Arabia have an agreement governing the shared Al-Disi Aquifer.[193] There are a few other regional agreements associated with information sharing and consultation regarding transboundary aquifers.[194] In each of these instances, however, the groundwater resource is treated distinctly from any surface water source. Similarly, most other international watercourse treaties focus, at least on their face, only on the management of surface waterbodies.

International framework treaties and proposed treaties are similarly bifurcated in nature. Over the course of the nearly twenty-five years of the UN's International Law Commission's (ILC) deliberations over the codification of the international water law, the scope of any framework treaty became a central point of debate.[195] The formulation of any framework treaty's scope ranged from 'successive international rivers' to 'river basins' to 'international drainage basin' to 'hydrographic basin.'[196] The very essence of international law lay at the center of this debate, as it was grounded in different conceptions of sovereignty.[197]

Some of the early ILC approaches to international water law appeared to integrate transboundary surface waters and groundwater. The International Law Association's 1966 Helsinki Rules defined the scope of international water

---

192 Acordo, supra note 82; see also Gabriel Eckstein, 'Hydraulic Harmony or Water Whimsy? Guarani Aquifer Countries Sign Agreement,' International Water Law Project Blog (August 5, 2010), http://www.internationalwaterlaw.org/blog/2010/08/05/hydraulic-harmony-or-water-whimsy-guarani-aquifer-countries-sign-agreement/.

193 Agreement Between the Government of the Hashemite Kingdom of Jordan and the Government of the Kingdom of Saudi Arabia for the Management and Utilization of the Ground Waters of the Al-Sag/Al-Disi Layer (April 20, 2015), http://www.internationalwaterlaw.org/documents/regionaldocs/Disi_Aquifer_Agreement-English2015.pdf.

194 See, e.g., Programme for the Development of a Regional Strategy for the Utilisation of the Nubian Sandstone Aquifer System—Terms of Reference for the Monitoring and Exchange of Groundwater Information of the Nubian Sandstone Aquifer System (October 5, 2000); Convention on the Protection, Utilisation, Recharge and Monitoring of the Franco-Swiss Genevois Aquifer (January 1, 2008).

195 Gabriel Eckstein, 'A Hydrogeological Perspective on the Status of Groundwater Resources under the UN Watercourse Convention,' *Columbia Journal of Environmental Law*, Vol. 30(2), pp. 525–564 (2005), pp. 525–532.

196 Ibid.

197 Ibid.

law principles as the 'drainage basin.'[198] 'Drainage basin' was formulated rather broadly to include a 'system of waters' that flowed to a 'common terminus.'[199] This scope appears to include both surface water and groundwater, at least to the extent that they are part of the same system and drain to the same point. Many ILC members, in deliberations over the framework treaty, agreed that this was the most scientifically defensible approach as it avoids the types of arbitrary line-drawing between surface water and groundwater that gave rise to the disputes seen in Arizona and between Nebraska and Kansas.[200]

International water law thus appeared, at least at those early stages, to have avoided the bifurcated system mistake that continues to vex the interstate water law in the United States. However, when the ILC finalized the Watercourse Convention in 1997, its scope was defined by the relevant 'watercourse,' which means a 'system of surface waters and groundwater constituting by virtue of their physical relationship a unitary whole and normally flowing into a common terminus' with parts located in different nations.[201] This definition appears to integrate groundwater, particularly as it expressly references groundwater.

However, there are at least some important groundwater resources that may not be covered by the Watercourse Convention. Fully-confined aquifers with no hydrologic connection to an identifiable surface water source are not part of a 'unitary whole' of the overlying system, and are not covered by the Watercourse Convention.[202] This may exclude such strategically important, and potentially highly-contested, groundwater sources as the Nubian Sandstone Aquifer shared between Chad, Egypt, Libya, and Sudan, and the Al-Disi Aquifer shared between Jordan and Saudi Arabia.[203] Even aquifers that are largely confined, but have a recharge zone that traverses international boundaries, are arguably excluded from the Watercourse Convention.[204] Such aquifers may include the Mountain Aquifer, shared between Israel and the Palestinian Territories, the Syr Darya Basin of Central Asia, and the Guarani Aquifer.[205]

---

198 International Law Association, Helsinki Rules on the Uses of the Waters of International Rivers and Comments, *Report of the Fifty-Second Conference* (1966), art. II.

199 Ibid.

200 Eckstein, supra note 195, p. 532.

201 UN Watercourses Convention, supra note 44, art. 2.

202 Eckstein, supra note 195, pp. 550–551.

203 Ibid.

204 Ibid.

205 Ibid.

Perhaps the greatest evidence of the limitations of the current approach of international water law with respect to managing groundwater resources, and the risk of water rights bifurcation in international law, is the ongoing debate and formulation of the Bellagio Draft Treaty.[206] This draft treaty is an attempt to establish an integrated international water rights regime, and is born out of ongoing disputes over groundwater between the United States and Mexico.[207] Water rights between the United States and Mexico are explicitly bifurcated, as there is no established treaty dealing directly and permanently with transboundary groundwater; the existing water allocation treaties provide only raw water allocations of shared surface water sources under the 1944 Rivers Treaty governing the Colorado River and Rio Grande/Rio Bravo.[208]

The Bellagio Draft Treaty provides some potential avenues to avoid bifurcation and the costs it imposes. For example, the Bellagio Draft Treaty relies on the concept of reasonable and equitable utilization, similar to the Watercourse Convention, and is also based on the broadly shared heritage of reasonableness associated with groundwater management under Roman and British law.[209] The Bellagio Draft Treaty also encourages the establishment of a database for information sharing regarding hydrologic parameters.[210] The draft also includes recommendations associated with dispute resolution, drought management, and even integrates groundwater quality protection.[211] The water quality protection element is particularly important for many of the aquifers that would otherwise be excluded from the scope of the Watercourse Convention, as these may be confined aquifers with limited recharge, and thus more susceptible to persistent contamination without the benefits of dilution or transport.[212] International water law may avoid at least some of the challenges of bifurcation that the United States faces by incorporating the approach embodied in the Bellagio Draft Treaty.

International water law can look to the United States to see the costs of legal bifurcation of water rights, but can also look at those same cases for

206 See generally Robert D. Hayton & Albert E. Utton, 'Transboundary Groundwaters: The Bellagio Draft Treaty,' *Natural Resources Journal*, Vol. 29(3), pp. 663–722 (1989).

207 Marilyn C. O'Leary, 'The Bellagio Draft Treaty as a Tool for Solving Border Groundwater Issues,' *U.S.-Mexico Law Journal*, Vol. 11(1), pp. 57–60 (2003).

208 1944 Rivers Treaty, supra note 82.

209 Amy Hardberger, 'What Lies Beneath: Determining the Necessity of International Groundwater Policy Along the United States-Mexico Border and a Roadmap to an Agreement,' Texas Tech Law Review, Vol. 35(1), pp. 1211–1258 (2004), pp. 1211–1258.

210 Ibid., p. 1233.

211 Hayton & Utton, supra note 206.

212 Eckstein, supra note 195, p. 545.

possible lessons on alleviating the costs of bifurcation. While the dispute over groundwater pumping between Kansas and Nebraska illustrates the folly of bifurcation that may impact international water law, the case also illustrates a possible approach to mitigate that folly. The special master appointed by the U.S. Supreme Court recommended disgorgement to address inequitable water allocations caused by Nebraska's willful over-pumping.[213] Effectively, the special master in the case found that Nebraska had knowingly violated its settlement with Kansas regarding well pumping impacting the Republican River, and thus the special master recommended a punitive payment—beyond real damages—of $1.8 million to be paid by Nebraska to Kansas.[214] Because the water had a higher value to Nebraska farmland than in Kansas, the situation was, as noted by Justice Elena Kagan, a 'recipe for breach.'[215] Disgorgement (the punitive payment) was thus fair in order to discourage willful breach.[216]

Integration of surface water and groundwater in transboundary water treaties is the preferred approach to avoiding the protracted disputes and arbitrary line-drawing associated with bifurcated regimes in the United States. However, where integration is not politically feasible, nations and international adjudicative bodies could agree to some form of offsets or use forebearance as an approximation of the disgorgement remedy. While this would not result in ideal integration, it would at least discourage over-pumping from shallow wells drilled near a river governed by an international treaty and the subsequent claim that such pumping is outside the scope of the treaty.

B *Characterizing Water as an Article of Commerce*

The issue of the legal bifurcation of surface water and groundwater is only one example of a persistent challenge of both domestic and international water law. Water does not lend itself well to line-drawing. Water is a part of everything, embedded as 'virtual water' in all goods and services.[217] Where 'water' as a subject of water law ends and 'virtual water' as a subject of commercial law begins is a problematic distinction to say the least. This distinction has proved difficult to make in inter-state commercial law in the United States.

---

213 *Kansas v. Nebraska*, supra note 190.

214 Ibid.

215 Ibid.

216 Ibid.

217 J. A. Allan, 'Virtual Water—The Water, Food, and Trade Nexus: Useful Concept or Misleading Metaphor?,' *Water International*, Vol. 28(1), pp. 106–113 (2003), p. 106.

The U.S. Constitution grants Congress the exclusive authority to regulate inter-state commerce.[218] This authority includes an implicit limit on the power of states to interfere with inter-state commerce—what is referred to as the Dormant Commerce Clause.[219] Where state regulation of inter-state commerce discriminates against other states—on its face or in effect, the regulation is subject to strict scrutiny by courts.[220] If the regulation is facially non-discriminatory, but nevertheless burdens inter-state commerce, courts apply a less stringent standard, upholding the regulation 'unless the burden imposed on [inter-state] commerce is clearly excessive in relation to the putative local benefits.'[221]

Water is unique in the United States in how its movement is regulated between states under the Dormant Commerce Clause.[222] States frequently seek to export water from neighboring states, and those states often erect legal barriers to prevent such water exports.[223] The U.S. Supreme Court upheld New Jersey's 1908 ban on such water exports in *Hudson County Water Co. v. McCarter*.[224] In that case, the Court held that 'few public interests are more obvious, indisputable and independent of particular theory than the interest of ... a State to maintain the rivers that are wholly within it substantially undiminished, except by such drafts upon them as the guardian of the public welfare may permit for the purpose of turning them to a more perfect use.'[225] Essentially, the Court held that state regulations aimed at protecting in-state water resources from out-of-state water users' appropriation constitute a valid exercise of the state's police power and is thus consistent with the Dormant

218 U.S. Constitution, art. I, § 8, cl. 3.

219 See, e.g., *United Haulers Association, Inc. v. Oneida-Herkimer Solid Waste Management Authority*, 550 U.S. 330, 338 (2007).

220 In *Hughes v. Oklahoma*, the Court states that 'the burden falls on the State to justify [the regulation] both in terms of the local benefits flowing from the statute and the unavailability of alternatives adequate to preserve the local interests at stake.' 441 U.S. 322, 336 (1979).

221 *Pike v. Bruce Church*, 397 U.S. 137, 142 (1970).

222 See generally Christine A. Klein, 'The Dormant Commerce Clause and Water Export: Toward a New Analytical Paradigm,' *Harvard Environmental Law Review*, Vol. 35(1), pp. 131–154 (2011).

223 See *Tarrant Regional Water District v. Herrmann*, 133 S. Ct. 2120 (2013) [*Tarrant*]; see also Complaint at 2–7, *Wind River Resources LLC v. Frisby*, No. 2:08-cv-00653-KJD-GWF (D. Nev. May 21, 2008).

224 *Hudson County Water Co. v. McCarter*, 209 U.S. 349 (1908).

225 Ibid., at 357–358.

Commerce Clause, thereby effectively excluding surface water flows from characterization as an 'article of commerce.'[226]

The U.S. Supreme Court cast a cloud of uncertainty over its own holding in *Hudson County* in 1982, when it decided *Sporhase v. Nebraska*.[227] In that case, the Supreme Court struck down a Nebraska state restriction on groundwater exports on Dormant Commerce Clause grounds.[228] A farmer owned land straddling the Colorado/Nebraska border, and sought a permit to withdraw groundwater from his land in Nebraska to irrigate crops located on his contiguous land located in Colorado.[229] Nebraska's denial of the permit was based on a statute granting the state discretion to deny permits for inter-state groundwater export that the state deems to be (1) unreasonable, (2) contrary to groundwater conservation, (3) detrimental to the public welfare, or (4) to states that do not grant reciprocal rights to export groundwater to Nebraska.[230] The U.S. Supreme Court upheld Nebraska's denial based on the first three justifications, but struck down the denial based on the reciprocity requirement as an unconstitutional burden on inter-state commerce.

The Court's decision in *Sporhase* raised many questions. First, it is unclear to what extent the decision overruled existing precedent on the Dormant Commerce Clause upholding water export restrictions, such as in *Hudson County*. Additionally, perhaps the Supreme Court was distinguishing between surface water and groundwater, holding that groundwater, unlike surface water, is an article of commerce. It is also possible that the unique facts of *Sporhase* (a single property owner whose land straddled the jurisdictional boundary) made the decision not generalizable to other inter-state water export cases.[231]

The U.S. Supreme Court cases involving water in inter-state commerce illustrate one of the central challenges of transboundary water management. Among natural resources, water is unique. Water is in some respects like other resources such as gold or oil—a valuable commodity with a global market. However, water is different in important ways. People do not squirt oil at each other in the summer or throw gold at each other in the winter, or baptize their children in petroleum. Water has unique aesthetic, cultural, and ecological

---

226 Tarlock, supra note 9, p. 381; Frank J. Trelease, 'State Water and State Lines: Commerce in Water Resources,' *University of Colorado Law Review*, Vol. 56(4), pp. 347–379 (1985).

227 458 U.S. 941 (1982) [*Sporhase*].

228 *Sporhase*, ibid.; see also Klein, supra note 222.

229 *Sporhase*, ibid.; see also Christine A. Klein, 'The Environmental Commerce Clause,' *Harvard Environmental Law Review*, Vol. 27(1), pp. 1–70 (2003).

230 *Sporhase*, ibid.; see also Nebraska Revised Statutes § 46–613.01.

231 See Klein, supra note 222; see also Klein, supra note 229.

importance, and is essential to all life on earth. If a nation loads a tanker with wheat or oil and ships it to a foreign country, that shipment represents open trade, a wealth of natural resources, and evidence of economic development. On the other hand, if you load the same tanker with fresh water and ship that water to a foreign country, it can be perceived as environmentally irresponsible, culturally insensitive, and a sacrifice of national security.[232] As such, international bulk water exports are controversial in ways that exports of other natural resources are not. The same is true in inter-state commerce in the U.S.—there is no question that natural gas is an article of commerce subject to the Dormant Commerce Clause. But water—because of its role in public health and welfare—can be a legitimate subject of regulation and restriction in inter-state commerce under a state's police power, if exercised to protect its own citizens.

The complexity of water in commerce can be better understood through the concept of virtual water. Virtual water is the water embedded in all products.[233] Significant amounts of virtual water are embedded in energy and food.[234] For example, the production of a single kilogram of wheat requires approximately 1,000 liters of water.[235] If 1,000 m^3 is exported as virtual water embedded in wheat or bottled in wine, there is no question of how the water is characterized commercially—it is an article of commerce under domestic inter-state U.S. commercial law, and certainly a good under international trade law. If that same quantity of water moves between two nations or two states in a natural watercourse, there is no question how the law characterizes that water. It is subject to transboundary water laws like transboundary water treaties in the international context, or inter-state compacts in the domestic U.S. context. If water is moved between states or nations in pipelines or tankers, the legal characterization of the water becomes more complex, and the political palatability of the commercial transaction more fraught.

If a nation exports water faster than it can be naturally recharged, then despite the hydrologic cycle's renewing effects, a nation may be depleting its

232 Rhett B. Larson, 'The Case of Canadian Bulk Water Exports,' *Canadian Global Affairs Institute* (2015), p. 5, https://d3n8a8pro7vhmx.cloudfront.net/cdfai/pages/609/attachments/original/1440452326/Canadian_Bulk_Water_Exports.pdf?1440452326.

233 Allan, supra note 217.

234 Ibid., p. 9.

235 World Water Council, 'E-Conference Synthesis: Virtual Water Trade—Conscious Choices,' *World Water Council* (2004), p. 3, http://www.waterfootprint.org/Reports/virtual_water_final_synthesis.pdf; see also A. Y. Hoekstra & A. K. Chapagain, 'Water Footprints of Nations: Water Use by People as a Function of Their Consumption Pattern,' *Water Resources Management*, Vol. 21(2), pp. 35–48 (2007), pp. 35–38.

water resources.[236] If laws allow water to be withdrawn from one basin and exported, then water is less likely to be recharged in its original basin, and the total amount of water may deplete over time.[237] This is often cited as the most significant sustainability concern associated with inter-basin water transfers, and ultimately the reason such exports meet public opposition and have laws against them based on public health and welfare.

The example of the Great Lakes illustrates the potential controversy associated with international water exports. The International Joint Commission (IJC) is the bilateral transboundary institution that implements treaty obligations between Canada and the United States regarding the shared Great Lakes, and refers to the lakes as a 'non-renewable resource' because less than one percent of the lakes' waters are renewed annually by precipitation.[238] The IJC has stated that the Great Lakes are fully allocated, meaning that if all claims to water in the Great Lakes are considered, 'there is never a 'surplus' of waters in the Great Lakes system.'[239]

Nevertheless, in 1998, a Canadian Company called the Nova Group secured a permit to export 600 million liters of water from Lake Superior via tanker to buyers in Asia.[240] Public opposition to that permit based on environmental and national security concerns resulted in the permit's revocation, and prompted the IJC to counsel against such bulk water exports from the Great Lakes basin.[241] More recently, the Canadian government licensed Canadian companies in British Columbia to export nearly 55.5 million cubic meters of water each year by tanker.[242] A Canadian company called Snowcap received one such license, and contracted with a U.S. company, called Sun Belt, to export water from British Columbia to California.[243] As with the Nova Group transaction, the export of water met public opposition and the government of

236 Hall & Cavataro, supra note 75, p. 1574.

237 Ibid., p. 1568; see also Kirt Mayland, 'Navigating the Murky Waters of Connecticut's Water Allocation Scheme,' *Quinnipiac Law Review*, Vol. 24(2), 685 (2006).

238 International Joint Commission, 'Protection of the Waters of the Great Lakes, Final Report 6,' *International Joint Commission* (2000) [IJC 2000 Report].

239 Ibid., p. 43.

240 Sandra Zellmer, 'The Anti-Speculation Doctrine and its Implications for Collaborative Water Management,' *Nevada Law Journal*, Vol. 8(3), pp. 994–1030 (2008), pp. 994–1001.

241 IJC 2000 Report, supra note 238, p. 46.

242 Terry L. Anderson & Clay J. Landry, 'Exporting Water to the World,' *Water Resources Update (Journal of Contemporary Water Research and Education)*, Vol. 118(1), pp. 60–67 (2001), pp. 60–62.

243 Paul S. Kibel, 'Grasp on Water: A Natural Resource that Eludes NAFTA's Notion of Investment,' *Ecology Law Quarterly*, Vol. 34(2), pp. 655–672 (2007), pp. 655–662.

British Columbia banned water exports and rescinded the permits like the one held by Snowcap.[244]

Both Sun Belt and Snowcap sued the British Columbia government for rescinding the water export licenses.[245] The provincial government settled with the Canadian Snowcap company.[246] Sun Belt, on the other hand, pursued a claim in Canadian federal court under Chapter 11 of the North American Free Trade Agreement (NAFTA).[247] Sun Belt sought $10.5 billion in damages, claiming that the provincial government violated the NAFTA Chapter 11 prohibition against signatory states treating domestic companies more favorably than companies from neighboring states, and prohibiting signatory states from limiting the free flow of goods between them.[248] Effectively, this case is the international corollary of the domestic questions involved in *Sporhase* and *Hudson County*—when is banning inter-basin water transfers between jurisdictions a valid exercise of police power to protect citizens and the environment, and when is it an unlawful interference with trade.

International trade law is similar in many respects to the laws under the Dormant Commerce Clause cases in the United States. Goods are defined under NAFTA and many other trade agreements with reference to how the term is used in the World Trade Organization's (WTO) General Agreement on Tariffs and Trade (GATT).[249] GATT does not define a 'good,' though it does state that a good must also be a 'product.' Under GATT, a product is '[s]omething produced by human or mechanical effort or by a natural process.' Under NAFTA, water flowing in natural streams, channels, or geologic formations is not a 'good' for purposes of international trade law, and is instead governed by international water treaties.[250] Water embedded in products as virtual water is a 'good.'[251] There is an ongoing debate regarding whether bulk water exported

244 Christopher S. Maravilla, 'The Canadian Bulk Water Moratorium and its Implications for NAFTA,' *Currents: International Trade Law Journal*, Vol. 10(1), pp. 29–35 (2001), pp. 29–32.

245 See Anderson & Landry, supra note 242, pp. 60–62.

246 Ibid.

247 Ibid.; see also North American Free Trade Agreement, December 8, 1993, 107 Stat. 2057, 32 I.L.M. 289, c. 11 [NAFTA].

248 Ibid.

249 Ibid., art. 201; General Agreement on Tariffs and Trade, October 30, 1947, 61 Stat. A-11, 55 *UNTS* 194 [GATT]; incorporated into NAFTA under NAFTA Article 309.

250 Edith Brown Weiss, 'Water Transfers and International Trade Law,' *in*, Edith Brown Weiss, Laurence Boisson de Chazournes & Nathalie Bernasconi-Osterwalder (eds.), *Fresh Water and International Economic Law*, pp. 61–92 (Oxford University Press, 2005).

251 Ibid.

by tanker or pipeline should be treated as a product or good under international trade law.[252]

Under international trade law, the characterization of water as a 'good' or 'product' is similar in legal consequence to characterizing water as an 'article of commerce' under U.S. inter-state commerce law. Under GATT and NAFTA, nations generally are prohibited from discriminating against the goods of other nations and from imposing restrictions on the import or export of goods.[253] The obligations assumed under GATT and other trade agreements are broad in their protections against such discrimination, with narrow exceptions allowed to address 'critical shortage' or to enact 'environmental measures necessary to protect human, animal or plant life or health [or] ... measures relating to the conservation of living and non-living exhaustible natural resources.'[254] A nation could claim one of these exceptions as the basis for banning bulk water exports.

The legal characterization of bulk water exports has important implications for global water management. If bulk water is a good, then nations will generally not be able to ban its export unless they avail themselves of one of the narrow exceptions for shortages or environmental or public health protection. If bulk water is not a good or product, then it lies outside the scope of international trade law and would have to be regulated, if at all, under an alternative approach. But just as a bifurcated water rights system draws an arbitrary distinction between surface water and groundwater, international trade law and domestic U.S. inter-state commerce law draw arbitrary lines between water in natural watercourses, virtual water, and bulk water exports in tankers or pipelines. The difficulty in reconciling *Sporhase* and *Hudson County* is perhaps at least partially caused by such arbitrary lines, and could foreshadow similar confusion in international trade law. The apparent contradiction between *Sporhase* and *Hudson County* would be resolved if water once removed from its natural watercourse—virtual or in-bulk—were treated as a good that is subject to inter-state commerce law, but which can be protected under claims of state police power.

Confusion could similarly be avoided in international law if water is treated as a good or product, whether virtual or bulk. Water in its natural watercourse would still be regulated under international water law treaties and customary international water law. But once removed from its natural watercourse, water could be treated as a good or product. This would avoid drawing arbitrary lines

252 Ibid.

253 Ibid.

254 Ibid.; NAFTA, supra note 247, art. 2101.

between the 1,000 liters of water bottled as wine, and the 1,000 liters of water moved by pipeline across an international border. Water is moving between countries either way, and placing it under international trade law eliminates an otherwise poorly-drawn distinction while placing bulk water exports clearly under international trade law.

While categorizing water as a good or product has potential risks associated with commodification of a critical and culturally-sensitive resource, such commodification can also be an important way to better value water. An efficient and well-regulated water market may facilitate internalization of the costs of water consumption to encourage conservation. Water is frequently wasted when consumers do not internalize the costs of consumption.[255] Water can be both a valuable commodity and a human right when it is appropriately valued, and when that value is reflected in affordable rates for basic human consumption and adequately accounts for the value of in-stream water to the environment.[256]

Additionally, international trade law can be implemented in ways that allow for efficient water markets while at the same time allowing sovereign states to protect resources for purposes of public health, welfare, drought resilience, and environmental protection. For large, inter-basin bulk water exports, the provisions of GATT and similar trade agreements would apply, including allowing exceptions discussed above associated with critical shortage, public health, and environmental protection. This would mean perhaps limiting bulk water exports of groundwater that exceeded the rate of the aquifer's natural recharge. Bulk water exports from surface water bodies would be limited to preserve in-stream flows.

Nations engaged in bulk water exports could rely on water footprint accounting to measure sustainability, that is, determining whether more water is being exported in both virtual and bulk categories than is being imported under those categories. This will give a more accurate picture of the impacts of water exports on national water security and how those exports might be offset through trade. The goals of water footprint accounting would be to promote water sustainability in all sectors, to limit overconsumption, and to encourage both national and global water security. Accounting for how water moves as virtual water between nations may allow for a clearer sense of how nations are achieving shared benefits in their cooperative management of transboundary basins. Each state would then reasonably and equitably share the 'benefits'

255 Rhett B. Larson, 'The New Right in Water,' *Washington & Lee Law Review*, Vol. 70(4), pp. 2181–2267 (2013), pp. 2181–2228.

256 Ibid.

of the shared watercourse as embodied in virtual water and as contemplated under Article 5 the Watercourse Convention.[257]

Such a shared benefits approach facilitates the integration of economic and socio-cultural considerations in transboundary water management. In striving to achieve shared benefits, outcomes should be evaluated not on the equity of raw water allocations, but upon equitable and efficient distributions of the benefits of water development, as embodied in water footprint accounting on the allocations of virtual water from the basin.[258] In this way, water embedded in energy and agricultural products is accounted for and integrated into evaluations of how a transboundary governing commission is distributing the benefits of water development in an international basin.

C *Accurate Data and Modelling in Water Rights Allocations*

As noted above, the Colorado River Compact allocated 7.5 million acre-feet per year to the upper basin states and 7.5 million acre-feet per year to the lower basin states.[259] Under the 1944 Rivers Treaty between the United States and Mexico, Mexico is allocated 1.5 million acre feet per year from the Colorado River.[260] The upper and lower basin allocations, when combined with Mexico's allocation and added to the 1.5 million acre-feet per year lost to evapotranspiration each year equal an assumed 18 million acre-feet available in the Colorado River each year.[261] These assumptions were based on data collected in the early 20th Century during flood years.[262] Recent studies including tree ring analysis indicate that the 1,000 year average amount of annual water available in the Colorado River is closer to 13 million acre-feet.[263] As such, the entire transboundary allocation framework of the Colorado River basin is based on potentially faulty assumptions about the quantity of water in the river. This would mean that the entire basin may be functioning perpetually in legal water shortage, regardless of drought-induced actual water shortage.[264]

---

257 UN Watercourses Convention, supra note 44, art. V.

258 Larson, supra note 255, p. 2228.

259 Colorado River Compact, supra note 78.

260 1944 Rivers Treaty, supra note 82.

261 Stacy Tellinghuisen, 'Water for Power Generation: What's the Value?,' *Natural Resources Journal*, Vol. 50(3), pp. 683–720 (2010), pp. 683–685.

262 Ludwik A. Teclaff, 'The River Basin Concept and Global Climate Change,' *Pace Environmental Law Review*, Vol. 8(2), pp. 355–388 (1991), pp. 355–376.

263 Gregory J. Hobbs, Jr., 'The Role of Climate in Shaping Western Water Institutions,' *University of Denver Water Law Review*, Vol. 7(1), pp. 1–46 (2003), FN 68.

264 Ibid.

The failure of the Colorado River Compact to be grounded on solid data has led to a structural deficit in the basin's inter-state water management regime. Because the allocations made by the U.S. Supreme Court in *Arizona v. California* are viewed by states, and by extension the citizens of these states, as vested water rights, the system has become legally rigid, with attempts to reallocate to address the structural deficit facing both political and legal challenges. The Secretary of the Interior's power to make shortage declarations has added some flexibility to the system, but at the cost of state sovereignty and the political legitimacy of the water rights allocation regime. This early failure to ground water allocations on sound data lies at the root of much of the ongoing transboundary political and legal struggles within the Colorado River basin.

Effective transboundary water management—whether at the domestic or international level—requires investment in solid data with good models and monitoring. Water policy should have the following priorities, in order: (1) understand what you have; (2) conserve what you have; (3) store what you have; and (4) if necessary, augment what you have. Too often jurisdictions will skip the first priority and invest resources in conversation or water augmentation without the critical first step of knowing just how much water needs to be conserved or augmented. That knowledge requires good data. One possible reform to avoid reliance on bad data and thus the institutionalization of structural deficits is an adaptive management regime.

Adaptive management is 'a systematic process for continually improving management policies and practices by learning from the outcomes of implemented management strategies.'[265] This approach requires allocation decisions to sunset at regular intervals and encourages reevaluation based on additional data, and then adaptation to new information if necessary. Adaptive management is especially effective in transboundary water management regimes where co-riparian jurisdictions collect, compare, share, and scrutinize data, including evaluating whether past successes or failures can be reproduced or

265 Claudia Pahl-Wostl, 'Transitions Towards Adaptive Management of Water Facing Climate and Global Change,' *Water Resource Management*, Vol. 21(1), pp. 49–62 (2007), pp. 49–51. Adaptive management is 'a decision process that promotes flexible decision making that can be adjusted in the face of uncertainties as outcomes from management actions and other events become better understood ... It is not a "trial by error" process, but rather emphasizes learning while doing.' B. K. Williams, R. C. Szaro & C. D. Shapiro, 'Adaptive Management: The U.S. Department of the Interior Technical Guide,' *Adaptive Management WorkingGroup, U.S. Department of the Interior* (2009), p. 4, https://www2.usgs.gov/sdc/doc/DOI-%20Adaptive%20ManagementTechGuide.pdf.

avoided or if they are attributable to unique temporal or spatial conditions. This adaptive management approach requires regular review of allocation decisions with external expert auditors to provide a critical evaluation of the data and modelling employed in making transboundary water appropriation decisions.

For example, a treaty regime capable of adapting to improved climate and hydrologic modeling in an international basin could adjust to a better understanding of predicted flows and avoid conflict during drought years.[266] Adaptive capacity in water treaties prevents approaches to water resource data collection and management from becoming stale and static by including regular review periods for data management within the treaty. Adaptive management ensures that information science in water management is state of the art.

Adaptive management should play a central role in all natural resource allocation regimes in the face of climate change, and has rightfully arisen to become the 'new paradigm for environmental and natural resource law in an age of climate change adaptation.'[267] But even disregarding its importance in responding to climate change, adaptive management serves to better respond to innovation as technology has advanced at an even more rapid rate than the climate has changed. Because adaptive management requires monitoring and response to new data and technologies, true adaptive management cannot be achieved without an institution facilitating information exchanges and monitoring the state of the art, like international river basin commissions.

Many international river treaties establish commissions that oversee allocation and development within international river basins. The nature of these commissions depends on the treaty, with some serving only as information sharing bodies and technical advisers, and some having monitoring and enforcement authority. One critical role these commissions should play is to ensure proper investment in monitoring and modelling technology in the basin, and accurate and transparent reporting of such data and modelling results between member states. These commissions should ensure that there is a regular review and requirement to update technologies, methodologies, and reporting requirements to adapt to changing hydrologic, climatologic, and technologic conditions.

One of the most important functions of good modelling, monitoring, and data reporting is to guide investment decisions within the basin. That is why

266 Larson, supra note 156, p. 759.

267 Robin Kundis Craig, '"Stationarity is Dead"—Long Live Transformation: Five Principles for Climate Change Adaptation Law,' *Harvard Environmental Law Review*, Vol. 34(1), pp. 9–73 (2009), pp. 9–18.

understanding available water resources and their condition is a higher priority even than conservation. Conservation can be costly, particularly when it requires fixing leaking pipes, lining ditches and canals, installing more efficient appliances and irrigation systems, or even in public education. A clearer picture of available water resources will guide inter-state commissions in understanding how much needs to be invested in conservation. More importantly, improved data and models will guide decisions of whether, and to what extent, commissions and their member states should invest in water augmentation, a typically even more costly endeavor than improved conservation.

Water augmentation can take several forms, ranging from traditional approaches like drilling more wells or building more reservoirs, to non-traditional approaches, like cloud seeding.[268] Inter-basin bulk water imports are another example of water augmentation.[269] Desalination is a growing form of water augmentation in many parts of the world.[270] And improved forestry management has also been relied on in some areas as a means of increasing stream flow.[271] Effective monitoring, modelling, and data reporting can allow transboundary water commissions to evaluate any shortfalls between supply and demand in the basin and conduct a cost-benefit analysis regarding investments in both conservation and augmentation. Costs associated with traditional approaches can include overdraft of limited groundwater resources and the environmental and social impacts associated with large dam constructions, including loss of critical habitat for endangered species and the dislocation of human communities.

Non-traditional approaches can have less well-established costs and benefits. Watershed management is one approach to potentially augment water supplies through the removal of vegetation from a basin's upland forests, including scrub brush or invasive species.[272] Watershed management can result in several benefits. First, vegetation removal can improve forest health by allowing other trees to reach full maturity.[273] Second, this removal may help avoid or mitigate wildfires and damaging insect infestations such as bark

268 Rhett B. Larson, 'Augmented Water Law,' *Texas Tech Law Review*, Vol. 48(3), pp. 757–781 (2016), pp. 757–775.

269 Ibid.

270 Ibid.

271 Ibid.

272 Diane E. McConkey, 'Federal Reserved Rights to Instream Flows in the National Forests,' *Virginia Environmental Law Journal*, Vol. 13(2), pp. 305–322 (1994), pp. 305–311; see also Brandon Loomis, 'Reduction in Tree Cover Over Rivers Could Mean More Water Flow,' *The Arizona Republic* (October 30, 2015).

273 McConkey, ibid.

beetles.[274] Third, improved forest health can decrease erosion and runoff, thereby improving water quality.[275] Fourth, forestry management within the basin can increase stream flow by removing vegetation that is taking up water that would otherwise reach the river, thereby augmenting water supplies.[276]

Healthy forests protect snowpack from melting too fast, and limit losses from evapotranspiration.[277] Forests affected by wildfires may expose more snow to evaporation and adversely impact water quality as runoff.[278] A basin commission's investment in improved forest health can increase water quantity and water quality.[279] Nevertheless, removal of vegetation can impact aquatic and wildlife habitat if done unsustainably by reducing shade cover, eliminating nesting areas, and increasing access by grazing animals to fragile river banks.[280] Furthermore, removal of scrub brush and immature trees can be costly with limited options for cost recovery, in part because the narrow trunk diameter of such vegetation does not lend itself well to timber use.[281] The creation of the right incentives to encourage forestry management will require improved basin-level data collection and recording.

As with forestry management, cloud seeding can also augment water supplies while raising difficult economic, environmental, and legal questions.[282]

---

274 Ibid. The ultimate effectiveness of watershed management in addressing wildfire concerns is the subject of intense scholarly debate. See generally Karen Bradshaw & Dean Lueck (eds.), *Wildfire Policy: Law and Economics Perspectives* (RFF Press, 2012).

275 McConkey, ibid.

276 Ibid.; see also Loomis, supra note 272.

277 Alden R. Hibbert, 'Water Yield Improvement Potential by Vegetation Management on Western Rangelands,' *Journal of American Water Resources Association*, Vol. 19(3), pp. 375–381 (1983).

278 Ibid.

279 Charles Troendle, Marc Wilcox, Greg Bevenger, & Laurie Porth, 'The Coon Creek Water Yield Augmentation Project: Implementation of Timber Harvesting Technology to Increase Streamflow,' *Forest Ecology and Management*, Vol. 143(1–3), pp. 179–187 (2001).

280 H. Michael Rauscher, 'Ecosystem Management Decision Support for Federal Forests in the United States: A Review,' *Forest Ecology and Management*, Vol. 114(2–3), pp. 173–197 (1999).

281 Elisabeth Long, '*Wyoming v. USDA*: A Look Down the Road at Management of Inventoried Roadless Areas for Climate Change Mitigation and Adaptation,' *Ecology Law Quarterly*, Vol. 40(2), pp. 329–383 (2013), pp. 329–341; but see Karen Bradshaw & Dean Lueck, 'Contracting for Control of Landscapes,' *Iowa Law Review*, Vol. 100(6), pp. 2507–2549 (2015) (discussing the incentives some forest landowners have to invest in watershed protection).

282 *Larson*, 268.

As such, as global temperatures rise, more water will be held in clouds.[283] Technology like cloud seeding, which makes that water vapor accessible, may be an important part of water supply augmentation. There are multiple different approaches to cloud seeding, but each usually involves aerial dispersal of particles (usually silver iodide or frozen carbon dioxide) that facilitate condensation and raindrop formation.[284] The viability of cloud seeding as an augmentation strategy depends on many factors, but studies show that seeding is effective and can induce an additional 5–25% precipitation from clouds.[285] A recent study in the Colorado River basin indicated a 5–15% increase in precipitation.[286]

But cloud seeding has potential costs as well. The image of aircraft spraying silver iodide particles into the air understandably raises environmental concerns, including the potential for bioaccumulation of silver in the environment.[287] Cloud seeding also raises concerns for human safety. For example, the U.S. military used cloud seeding as a tactical weapon for its war effort in Vietnam from 1967 to 1972, in what was called 'Operation Popeye.'[288] The controversial effectiveness of this operation eventually led to the International Convention on the Prohibition of Military or Any Other Hostile Use of Environmental Modification Techniques of 1977 ('ENMOD').[289] The ratification of ENMOD indicates the risks of flood damage induced by cloud seeding.[290]

Desalination, while not as experimental as cloud seeding, also raises important questions of costs and benefits requiring careful monitoring and modelling across the basin. Membrane desalination requires either an electrically-charged or pressure gradient to move water or salt ions through a

---

283 Ibid.

284 Arnett S. Dennis, 'Weather Modification by Cloud Seeding,' *International Geophysics Series*, Vol. 24(3), 670 (1980).

285 Morteza Khalili Sr. et al., 'Results of Cloud Seeding Operations for Precipitation Enhancement in Iran during 1999–2007,' *Planned and Inadvertent Weather Modification/ Weather Modification Association* (April 22, 2008), http://ams.confex.com/ams/17WModWMA/techprogram/paper_13 9149.htm.

286 Ibid.

287 Erica C. Smit, 'Geoengineering: Issues of Accountability in International Law,' *Nevada Law Journal*, Vol. 15(2), pp. 1060–1089 (2015).

288 Noah Byron Bonnheim, 'History of Climate Engineering,' *Climate Change*, Vol. 1(4), pp. 891–897 (2010).

289 James R. Fleming, 'The Climate Engineers,' *The Wilson Quarterly*, Vol. 31(2), pp. 46–60 (2007).

290 Ibid.

membrane to separate salt and water.[291] Desalination's environmental impacts and the cost to avoid or mitigate those impacts pose obstacles to responsibly implementing the technology.[292] Desalination has potential environmental impacts, including the disposal of brine wastes and impacts on marine or aquatic ecosystems from intake valves.[293] But the economic and environmental costs associated with the high energy requirements for desalination remain its greatest obstacle to broad implementation.[294]

Those energy costs have historically been so high as to limit reliance on desalination to extremely water-poor but extremely energy-rich nations, such as Saudi Arabia.[295] However, technological advances in recent years have significantly decreased the energy costs. For example, photovoltaic solar energy has been implemented to lower desalination energy costs, and pressure transfer systems conserve energy by recycling pressure in brine waste streams to the production stream. [296] The combination of such technologies can decrease desalination costs.[297]

International river basin commissions will require reliable data to evaluate the costs, benefits, and demand for such augmentation technology. That evaluation should include comparing the costs and benefits of investments in augmentation with other measures, like limiting water loss by repairing leaking infrastructure. But these commissions will also have to answer legal questions regarding international rights to augmented supplies. If one country invests

---

291 Ibid.

292 R. Campbell & A. Jones, 'Appropriate Disposal of Effluent from Coastal Desalination Facilities,' *Desalination*, Vol. 182(1), pp. 365–372 (2005).

293 Tamim Younos, 'Environmental Issues of Desalination,' *Journal of Contemporary Water Research & Education*, Vol. 132(1), pp. 11–18 (2005).

294 Larson, supra note 268.

295 See generally Walid A. Abderrahman, 'Energy and Water in Arid Developing Countries: Saudi Arabia, A Case-Study,' *International Journal of Water Resources Development*, Vol. 17(2), pp. 247–255 (2010).

296 Y. M. El-Sayed, 'The Rising Potential of Competitive Solar Desalination,' *Desalination*, Vol. 216(1–3), pp. 314–324 (2007); see also Y. M. Kim et al., 'Overview of Systems Engineering Approaches for Large-Scale Seawater Desalination Plant with a Reverse Osmosis Network,' *Desalination*, Vol. 238(3), pp. 312–332 (2009); see, e.g., Tom<s Cazurra, 'Water Reuse of South Barcelona's Wastewater Reclamation Plant,' *Desalination*, Vol. 218(1), pp. 43–51 (2008).

297 Cazurra, ibid. For example, the desalination plant on the mouth of the Llobregat River in Barcelona, Spain relies on solar power, a pressure transfer system, and co-location with a wastewater treatment plant. These techniques have substantially reduced energy consumption from 25 kwH/m^3 typical of desalination plants in the 1980s to approximately 2.5 kwH/ m^3 today in the Barcelona plant.

in cloud seeding or forestry management, should that investment be factored into the allocation of the shared water resource? If not, the commission may discourage necessary investment in augmentation. But if such countries do have superior legal rights to augmented water, then international water law may inequitably favor wealthier nations with the resources to invest in augmentation technology over their less wealthy co-riparian neighbors. Must a nation that augments supplies through desalination forego diversions from a shared river to make more water available to a neighbor who cannot rely on desalination? If so, international water law may prevent adequate investment in a critical and evolving technology. Ultimately, the answer to these difficult legal questions will require accurate, up-to-date data and models in order to evaluate whether supplies are augmented and how technology has contributed to those augmented supplies. The evaluation of reasonableness and equity in light of investments in conservation and augmentation requires first a legal regime that encourages the sharing of reliable, up-to-date information regarding water resources in the basin.

D *Inappropriate Empowerment of Inter-State Water Commissions*

Effective sharing of reliable data across the basin will depend on the legitimacy of the international river basin commissions. But that legitimacy is difficult to achieve or to perceive whenever it threatens the sovereignty of member states. This sovereignty questions arises in inter-state river basin commissions in the United States. And these commissions have frequently failed to function as effective governing institutions without overstepping their bounds and threatening the sovereignty of their member states.

A recent U.S. Supreme Court's decision is illustrative of this challenge. In *Tarrant Regional Water District v. Herrmann*, decided in June of 2013, a Texas agency with the responsibility to provide water to farms and communities in north-central Texas filed for a permit from the Oklahoma Water Resources Board ('OWRB').[298] The permit would allow Texas to divert water from a point along a tributary of the Red River located within Oklahoma, and transfer that water across state boundaries into Texas.[299] The states of Oklahoma, Texas, Arkansas, and Louisiana signed the Red River Compact in 1978 to govern the shared Red River between the co-riparian states, and established the Red River Commission, made up of representatives of each member state, to implement

298 *Tarrant*, supra note 223.

299 Ibid.; see also Holly Taylor, 'Tarrant Regional Water District v. Herrmann: Interpreting Silence in Inter-state Water Compacts with Respect to State Boundaries and the Right to Access Water,' *University of Denver Water Law Review*, Vol. 17(1), pp. 138–155 (2013).

the compact and manage the river.[300] Oklahoma state law generally barred transboundary exports of water from the state, but Tarrant argued that the Red River Compact preempted state law and required equal access by all co-riparians to up to 25% of 'excess' waters (or 'unallocated waters').[301] Tarrant also argued that the Red River Compact's silence regarding transboundary water exports implicitly authorized such transfers.[302]

In its decision, the U.S. Supreme Court narrowly construed the Red River Compact, refusing to read into its silence an implicit guarantee of transboundary access to water.[303] The Supreme Court held that states do not cede sovereignty over natural resources absent clear and express statements within a compact, and that in any event, the Red River Commission had not adequately accounted for water in the basin, and thus no member states could clearly establish that there were any excess or unallocated waters.[304] If such an accounting demonstrated that there were unallocated waters, and Oklahoma's prohibition on water exports discriminated against water rights permit applicants from Texas, such discrimination might have violated constitutional principles governing inter-state commerce.[305] The weakness of the commission under the Red River Compact, evidenced by its failure to even provide an accounting of water resources, is typical of other inter-state commissions established by compacts in the United States.[306] The Red River Commission was underfunded and inadequately empowered in part because member states feared that a well-funded and empowered commission would threaten their sovereignty over water resources.

But an inter-state commission that is meaningfully empowered and well-funded may present other problems, including threatening the sovereignty of member states. For example, there is an ongoing controversy over hydraulic fracturing in the Delaware River basin involving the Delaware River Basin

300 *Tarrant*, ibid.; see also Act of December 22, 1980, Pub. L. No. 96–564, 94 Stat. 3305. The Red River is shared between the states of New Mexico, Texas, Oklahoma, Arkansas, and Louisiana.

301 *Tarrant*, ibid.; see also Taylor, supra note 299.

302 *Tarrant*, ibid. at 2136.

303 Ibid.

304 Ibid. at 2132–2136.

305 Ibid. at 2136–2137.

306 Grant Harse, 'Nebraska's Costs of Compliance with the Republican River Compact: An Equitable Solution,' *Kansas Journal of Law & Public Policy*, Vol. 19(1), pp. 124–147 (2009), pp. 124–131 (discussing the litigation involving the Republican River Compact and the role of courts in enforcing compact provisions).

Commission (DRBC).[307] The states of the Delaware River basin (Delaware, New Jersey, New York, and Pennsylvania) signed the Delaware River Basin Compact in 1961, and created the DRBC.[308] The DRBC is not limited to setting management goals or accounting for water allocations like other, weaker commissions, but has regulatory, permitting, and enforcement authority, and can also issue bonds.[309] The DRBC has been called 'one of the most powerful regional agencies ever created.'[310]

The DRBC issued a moratorium on the use of water within the Delaware River basin for hydraulic fracturing in 2009.[311] Hydraulic fracturing, or 'fracking,' is a method of natural gas production in which shale formations are fractured with the injection of high-pressure fluids to allow the recovery of natural gas.[312] Fracking has become a widely used but controversial means of energy production in the United States, in particular within the large Marcellus shale formation in the Delaware River basin.[313] Fracking is controversial for both water quantity and water quality reasons. Fracking requires as much as four million gallons of water for a single well.[314] Additionally, fracking fluids often contain hazardous chemicals, like benzene and formaldehyde, which can contaminate groundwater.[315] These concerns precipitated the DRBC's moratorium.[316]

In 2011, the DRBC proposed ending its moratorium on fracking within the Delaware River basin in the face of pressure from industry, legislators, and representatives of some of the commission's member states.[317] However, the

---

307 See generally The Delaware River Basin Compact, http://www.state.nj.us/drbc/library/documents/compact.pdf; see also Ian Urbina, 'Drilling Down: Regulation Lax as Gas Wells' Tainted Water Hits River,' *New York Times* (February 26, 2011), http://www.bctwa.org/FrkBC-DrillingDown-NewYorkTimes.pdf.

308 Delaware River Basin Compact, Pub. L. No. 87–328, 75 Stat. 688 (1961).

309 Larson, supra note 7, pp. 908–915.

310 Joseph L. Sax et al., *Legal Control of Water Resources, Cases and Materials* (4th ed.) (Thomson West, 2006), p. 854.

311 Craig, supra note 294, pp. 251–252.

312 Ibid., pp. 242–243.

313 Ibid.

314 Ibid., p. 252; see also Amy Hardberger, 'Powering the Tap Dry: Regulatory Alternatives for the Energy-Water Nexus,' *University of Colorado Law Review*, Vol. 84(3), pp. 529–579 (2013).

315 Craig, ibid., pp. 249–251; see also Rhett B. Larson, 'Reconciling Energy and Food Security,' *University of Richmond Law Review*, Vol. 48(4), pp. 929–958 (2014), pp. 929–944.

316 Craig, ibid., p. 252; see also Mark Squillace & Alexander Hood, 'NEPA, Climate Change, and Public Lands Decision Making,' *Environmental Law*, Vol. 42(2), pp. 469–526 (2012), pp. 505–506.

317 Laura Reeder, 'Creating a Legal Framework for Regulation of Natural Gas Extraction from the Marcellus Shale Formation,' *William & Mary Environmental Law & Policy Review*, Vol. 34(3), pp. 999–1026 (2010).

attorney general for the State of New York filed two different lawsuits against the DRBC, claiming that the commission did not conduct an environmental impact assessment for the lifting of the moratorium.[318]

The fracking controversy in the Delaware River basin illustrates the importance of establishing not only remedies against co-riparians under the inter-state river basin compact, but also potential remedies against the inter-state river basin commission itself. It is one thing for Texas to sue Oklahoma under the Red River Compact. But it is something else for New York to sue the DRBC. In the United States, state governments hold title to water within their boundaries, and hold that water in trust for the benefit of citizens.[319] States then grant usufructory water rights to their citizens consistent with that trust obligation, under either the riparian or prior appropriation approach to water rights.[320] There is no question that states owe a trust obligation toward their citizens in apportioning water rights. But the DRBC dispute raises the question of what obligation, if any, a commission owes to its member states in how it manages a transboundary watercourse. This is a particularly critical question when some members of a basin commission could be marginalized because they lack the economic resources or political influence of co-riparians in the commission. If Pennsylvania wants to develop shale gas through fracking, or New York wants to prevent it, but one is effectively precluded from doing so because the DRBC has been co-opted by the other, it is unclear what obligation the DRBC owes to the marginalized member state.

This problem is more pronounced in the Delaware River basin, where the commission is 'one of the most powerful regional agencies ever created.'[321] In that context, the commission could usurp state sovereignty without any legal check on such an abuse of its power by member states. New York's lawsuit against the DRBC raises the question of whether, and how, marginalized members of a basin commission could seek redress when the commission is not managing transboundary water for the benefit of all sharing jurisdictions.

318 Ibid.

319 Larson, supra note 7, pp. 908–915.

320 Abrams, supra note 26, p. 10437; see also Joseph L. Sax, 'The Limits of Private Rights in Public Waters,' *Environmental Law*, Vol. 19(2), pp. 473–483 (1989): Carol Rose, 'The Comedy of the Commons: Custom, Commerce, and Inherently Public Property,' *University of Chicago Law Review*, Vol. 53(3), pp. 711–781 (1986).

321 Sax et al., supra note 310, p. 854; see also Dellapenna (2005), supra note 3, p. 844 (stating that the DRBC has unusually expansive water management authority within the basin), for another example of strong interstitial federalism institutions [at least when compact provisions are enforced in court].

The controversy in the Red River basin illustrates how a weak river basin commission can give rise to cost-externalization (with Oklahoma externalizing costs of scarcity to Texas), economic and hydrologic protectionism (in light of Oklahoma's legal barriers to water exports), and protracted litigation without an effective inter-state dispute resolution forum.[322] The controversy in the Delaware River basin illustrates how a river basin commission with too much power can be perceived as a threat to state sovereignty.[323] Additionally, the DRBC's moratorium on fracking raises the question of how river basin commissions can avoid marginalizing members and provide means for all member states to ensure shared water are managed equitably and for the benefit of all.[324]

The Red River and Delaware River are examples of what might be called a 'Goldilocks governance challenge,' after the 'Goldilocks and the Three Bears' story where the little girl found one object too firm or hot, another too soft or cold, and the last 'just right.'[325] If the river basin commission has too little power, the basin is likely to see problems similar to those in the Red River basin, like externalities and protectionism. If the river basin commission is too powerful, or if there is too much power asymmetry between members of the commission due to the presence of a hydro-hegemon, then the basin is likely to see problems similar to those in the Delaware River basin, like member marginalization. Either scenario represents a failure to comply with the internalization prescription—to appropriately scale and empower a jurisdiction whose boundaries conform to the geography of the spillover commons like rivers.

This sort of challenge can be seen in international river basins as well. The Mekong River Commission, for example, constitutes a relatively empowered international commission with joint monitoring, oversight, and dispute resolution authority.[326] On the other hand, the treaty regime between Kazakhstan, Kyrgyzstan, and Uzbekistan governing the Syr Drya River provides for some

---

322 Kirsten Engel, 'State Environmental Standard-Setting: Is There a "Race" and is it "To the Bottom"?,' *Hastings Law Journal*, Vol. 48(3), pp. 271–398 (1997), pp. 271–285.

323 See Lisa Blomgren Bingham, 'The Next Generation of Administrative Law: Building the Legal Infrastructure for Collaborative Governance,' *Wisconsin Law Review*, Vol. 2010(2), pp. 297–356 (2010); see also Aaron-Andrew P. Bruhl, 'Hierarchically Variable Deference to Agency Interpretations,' *Notre Dame Law Review*, Vol. 89(2), pp. 727–784 (2013).

324 See Hasday, supra note 76, p. 26 (noting that state governments make little effort to integrate inter-state commissions into their own governance frameworks, leaving the onus on the inter-state commission to be inclusive and avoid marginalization of members).

325 Larson, supra note 7, pp. 908–920.

326 Jaroslav Tir & Douglas M. Stinnett, 'The Institutional Design of Riparian Treaties: The Role of River Issues,' *Journal of Conflict Resolution*, Vol. 55(4), pp. 606–631 (2011), p. 607.

dispute resolution, but otherwise does not authorize any international commission to engage in monitoring or enforcement.[327] Many other rivers, including major international rivers like the Euphrates, have no regional, multilateral treaty regime. How can international water law respond to the Goldilocks governance challenge, and appropriately empower international commissions under the internalization prescription without usurping national sovereignty?

The obstacle at the center of the Goldilocks governance challenge is political, not legal, in nature. Nations may oppose any sacrifice of sovereignty to a regional institution, particularly when there is a history of power asymmetries involved in sharing the watercourse. One possible approach to overcoming this political obstacle, however, is legal in nature. International river basin commissions could engage in fiduciary governance, established by treaty, to avoid marginalization of member nations, under which they would provide a remedy available to a member nation when the commission fails to reasonably manage the shared watercourse for the benefit of all members.[328] Such an approach would be similar to the trust relationship U.S. states hold to their citizens with respect to water management, but scaled up to the international, transboundary level.[329]

Implicit within that trust relationship is a corresponding fiduciary obligation to manage water resources reasonably and with a good faith effort to distribute benefits equitably between member nations. Where the international commission fails to adequately integrate the participation and views of member states, where it fails to reasonably and equitably manage shared resources, or where management decisions are shown to be arbitrary, capricious, or not in accordance with the governing treaty, member states could have a cause of action against the commission itself. Such a cause of action based on a breach of fiduciary duty is common in countries that recognize the public trust doctrine.[330] This approach allows member states some level of oversight and

327 Ibid.

328 See generally Ethan J. Leib, David L. Ponet & Michael Serota, 'A Fiduciary Theory of Judging,' *California Law Review*, Vol. 101(3), pp. 699–753 (2013); see also Ethan J. Leib, David L. Ponet, & Michael Serota, 'Translating Fiduciary Principles into Public Law,' *Harvard Law Review Forum*, Vol. 126(3), pp. 91–101 (2013); but see Seth Davis, 'The False Promise of Fiduciary Government,' *Notre Dame Law Review*, Vol. 89(3), pp. 1145–1207 (2014).

329 Michael D. Morrison & Keith Dollahite, 'The Public Trust Doctrine: Insuring the Needs of Texas Bays and Estuaries,' *Baylor Law Review*, Vol. 37(3), pp. 365–424 (1985); Craig, supra note 91, p. 53; Joseph L. Sax, 'The Public Trust Doctrine in Natural Resource Law: Effective Judicial Intervention,' *Michigan Law Review*, Vol. 68(1), pp. 471–566 (1970), pp. 471–477.

330 Michael C. Blumm & Rachel D. Guthrie, 'Internationalizing the Public Trust Doctrine: Natural Law and Constitutional and Statutory Approaches to Fulfilling the Saxion

a check against overreach and the usurpation of sovereignty where the commission itself acts against the interests of member states in managing water resources.

Of course, there are many challenges to implementing such a fiduciary relationship within an international basin commission, including the risk that it will aggravate conflict rather than facilitate cooperation. Breach of duty claims within the commission could potentially become either unenforceable affairs of political posturing, or protracted and costly approaches to dispute resolution, without effective enforcement mechanisms and efficient procedures.[331] And, of course, fiduciary governance will not solve all inter-jurisdictional disputes within a basin. However, the inability of a fiduciary to satisfy all of the beneficiaries of the trust is not necessarily a reason to abandon fiduciary obligations entirely. Co-riparian nations could use such a cause of action to stall or manipulate water management decisions, but the value of this cause of action as an inducement to cooperation would ideally outweigh potential costs.

However, mistrust of co-riparian states and their ability to capture interstitial federalism institutions could result in holdouts in the compact negotiation process, which would unnecessarily increase transaction costs and thwart many of the benefits of interstitial federalism.[332] States have options, however, that can be included within the compact to counter the problem of holdouts and avoid protracted litigation over the fiduciary duties of interstitial federalism institutions.

International politics could rob commission of their potential to facilitate collaborative governance in other ways. Many parts of nations that are parties to international river treaties lie outside of the river basin, and yet would have some representation on a river basin commission. This could increase transactions costs associated with negotiations and dispute resolution by incorporating remote, disengaged stakeholders into the governance of the basin. One potential solution to this problem is to treat the trust relationship as

---

Vision,' *UC Davis Law Review*, Vol. 45(3), pp. 741–808 (2012); *Arkansas Democrat-Gazette v. Zimmerman*, 20 S.W.3d 301, 304 (Ark. 2000).

331 Ryan Rowberry, 'Drinking from the Same Cup: Federal Reserved Water Rights and National Parks in the Eastern United States,' *Georgia State University Law Review*, Vol. 29(4), pp. 987–1023 (2013), pp. 987–1020; Joseph W. Girardot, 'Toward a Rational Scheme of Inter-state Water Compact Adjudication,' *University of Michigan Journal of Legal Reform*, Vol. 23(1), pp. 151–177 (1989), pp. 151–152.

332 Jonathan B. Wiener, 'Global Environmental Regulation: Instrument Choice in Legal Context,' *Yale Law Journal*, Vol. 108(2), pp. 677–800 (1999), pp. 677–741; see also Stephen N. Bretsen & Peter J. Hill, 'Water Markets as a Tragedy of the Anti-Commons,' *William & Mary Environmental Law & Policy Review*, Vol. 33(3), pp. 723–783 (2009), pp. 723–744.

one between the river basin commission and the people of the basin itself. Commission membership could be limited to government officials representing solely interests from within the basin. This would obviously involve difficult line-drawing exercises, but would also limit the circumstances in which one member state could bring a breach of fiduciary duty against the commission to only those scenarios where the interest of residents of the basin are directly implicated.

This proposal regarding a trust relationship is broad in both geographic scope and in its policy implications, with serious obstacles to implementation. But it has potential advantages to address the Goldilocks governance challenge and comply with the cost internalization prescription. Part of the benefit of this approach is to strike a balance between policies resulting in a tragedy of the commons (lack of clearly defined property rights resulting in negative externalities) or the tragedy of the anti-commons (over-assignment of private property rights resulting in high transaction costs).[333] Where a resource like water is inherently common-pool and spill-over, a single trustee can manage the resource for the benefit of all within the pool to lower transaction costs while recognizing the rights of individual states, thereby striking an appropriate middle ground between the two potential tragic outcomes.

National water rights under treaty, whether raw water allocations or based on reasonable and equitable utilization, still ensure some measure of excludability to limit the risks of the tragedy of the commons, but a commission's oversight can lower transaction costs and avoid the tragedy of the anti-commons.[334] Perhaps even more importantly, the public trust doctrine at the international commission level could play an effective role in protecting common property by encouraging collaboration and inter-cultural understanding.[335] This is perhaps the highest aim of the international basin commission—a deeper sense of collaborative governance of the shared water resource that, by nature, defies strict private property regimes. This public trust approach could strike the right balance in the Goldilocks governance challenge and satisfy the internalization prescription for spillover commons, like water.

But meeting the Goldilocks governance challenge and complying with the internalization prescription is only one aim of transboundary water

333 See Michael A. Heller, 'The Boundaries of Private Property,' *Yale Law Journal*, Vol. 108(2), pp. 1163–1223 (1999), pp. 1163–1168.

334 Barton H. Thompson, Jr., 'The Public Trust Doctrine: A Conservative Reconstruction & Defense,' *Southeastern Environmental Law Journal*, Vol. 15(1), pp. 47–70 (2006).

335 Ibid., p. 63; see also Rose, supra note 320, p. 711.

governance. The other is to achieve integrated water resource management (IWRM), or what might be called the integration prescription for governing spillover commons.[336] IWRM is a process requiring coordinated development and management of water across different economic, social, and ecological interests without compromising sustainability and environmental protection.[337] There are three considerations essential for effective integration in transboundary water management: (1) economic integration; (2) socio-political integration; and (3) ecological integration.

First, international river basin commissions should integrate the economic considerations of water resource management. Greater integration of economic considerations could be achieved through water footprint monitoring and reporting for a clearer understanding of how water moves through and out of the basin as virtual water.[338] As noted above, the failure to account for virtual water makes for ambiguous and sometimes arbitrary distinctions in water resource management.[339] Basin commissions that focus on raw water apportionment or on information sharing, but fail to integrate questions of water efficiency in energy production or crop irrigation, cannot manage the resource consistent with any kind of trust obligation because the lines distinguishing where the managed resource begins and ends are ill-defined.

Second, international river basin commissions should integrate socio-cultural considerations into transboundary water management. This is difficult given water's unique religious, aesthetic, cultural, and recreational values, and how those values vary across the basin.[340] The challenge of socio-cultural integration into water management decisions is exacerbated in the current model of interstitial federalism by a narrow, exclusionary approach to commission membership, which might be better addressed through greater participation of indigenous communities in commission management decisions and deliberations. Other groups may also be integrated into management decisions in order to better represent socio-cultural values of water. Municipalities, nongovernmental organizations, and public utilities often play important roles in

---

336 Larson, supra note 255, p. 2228.

337 Ibid.; see also Barton H. Thompson, Jr., 'A Federal Act to Promote Integrated Water Management: Is the CZMA a Useful Model?,' *Environmental Law*, Vol. 42(1), pp. 201–240 (2012), pp. 201–213.

338 See, e.g., Allan, supra note 217, p. 4; see also J. A. Allan, 'Virtual Water—Part of an Invisible Synergy that Ameliorates Water Scarcity,' *in*, Peter Rogers, Ramon Llamas, & Luis Martinez-Cortina (eds.), *Water Crisis: Myth or Reality*, pp. 131–150 (Taylor & Francis, 2006) (virtual water is water embedded in commodities like food, energy, and clothing).

339 See *Sporhase*, supra note 227, at 940–950.

340 Ibid. at 949; see also Larson, supra note 174, p. 81.

the development and conservation of water resources in a basin and can provide a greater range of perspectives on the cultural values of water.[341]

Third, international river basin commissions should include ecological considerations into water resource management. This should include greater integration of water quality issues, critical habitat, and biodiversity in water management decisions. For example, the invasive Asian Carp in the Great Lakes basin represents perhaps a greater basin-level threat than drought or over-appropriation.[342] Yet the impacts on species lie outside the scope of the Great Lakes Treaty and the International Joint Commission's jurisdiction. Jurisdiction over endangered species in the Great Lakes is drawn too broadly to minimize transaction costs and move expeditiously to address the imminent threat of Asian Carp, or too narrowly, leading to the externalities of invasive species like Asian Carp in the first place. Thus the current model of transboundary water management too often fails to adequately address the Goldilocks governance challenge with respect to the protection of the environment.

International river basin commissions that satisfy the internalization and integration prescriptions for effective transboundary water management are not necessarily a threat to national sovereignty if constrained by a fiduciary obligation to member nations. The commissions must be funded by member nations to a degree that they can be the clearinghouse for relevant data on the basin, employ technical experts, and internalize costs through effective oversight and lower transaction costs by facilitating efficient dispute resolution.[343] International river basin commissions must move beyond the limited functions of pure gross allocation or pure information sharing to true integrated water resource management, and assume the primary jurisdictional role over inter-state waters appropriately constrained by principles of fiduciary governance.

---

341 See, e.g., Laura Pedraza-Fariña, 'Conceptions of Civil Society in International Lawmaking and Implementation: A Theoretical Framework,' *Michigan Journal of International Law*, Vol. 34(3), pp. 605–673 (2013); J. B. Ruhl, 'General Design Principles for Resilience and Adaptive Capacity in Legal Systems—With Application to Climate Change Adaptation,' *North Carolina Law Review*, Vol. 89(5), pp. 1373–1403 (2011).

342 See generally David A. Strifling, 'An Ecosystem Based Approach to Slowing the Synergistic Effects of Invasive Species and Climate Change,' *Duke Environmental Law & Policy Forum*, Vol. 22(1), pp. 145–193 (2011); Molly M. Watters, 'Fish and Federalism: How the Asian Carp Litigation Highlights a Deficiency in the Federal Common Law Displacement Analysis,' *Michigan Journal of Environmental & Administrative Law*, Vol. 2(2), pp. 535–562 (2013).

343 See Zachary L. McCormick, 'Inter-state Water Allocation Compacts in the Western United States—Some Suggestions,' *Water Resources Bulletin*, Vol. 30(3), pp. 385–395 (1994), pp. 385–390.

Conclusion

The management of transboundary waters represents a complex amalgam of political, economic, and legal issues. When these water resources are scarce or highly variable—as they are in many parts of the world or are more likely to become in the face of global climate change—their management becomes all the more difficult. Nations may become more protectionist over resource over which they claim sovereignty and more belligerent in asserting that sovereignty when something as critical as water is at stake. Laws and legal institutions aimed at managing transboundary waters must attempt to thread the needle of the Goldilocks governance challenge by being strong enough to internalize costs and integrate the myriad considerations implicated by water policy, but not so strong as to discourage participation or marginalized members. Their geographic scope must be broad enough to encompass the basin and effectively integrate its economic, socio-cultural, and environmental considerations, but not so broad that the transaction costs associated with management stifle innovation and dialogue.

The United States has nearly two centuries of experimentation in transboundary water management between its sovereign subsidiary states. The social, cultural, linguistic, economic, political, and legal differences between these subsidiary states obviously do not approach the variability seen across an international basin. Thus, inter-state water law is far from a perfect comparison to international water law. Nevertheless, those two centuries of experience in attempting to comply with the internalization and integration prescriptions for water policy and meet the Goldilocks governance challenge have provided useful examples of both successes and failures in transboundary water management.

International law alone cannot overcome international politics or historic rivalries over transboundary resources. A complete solution may prove elusive, and will certainly require more than mere legal reforms. But inter-state water law in the United States suggests some legal reforms that at least begin to address the Goldilocks governance challenge. The success of considering shared domestic water law principles in making a determination of reasonableness and equity in transboundary water rights provides a common foundation upon which to build an inter-jurisdictional legal regime. The recognition of the rights of indigenous peoples encourages the equitable treatment of these communities while integrating their expertise and socio-cultural values. The reliance on special masters, while politically-fraught, has nevertheless been an important spur to encourage inter-jurisdictional cooperation and greater institutional competency in water rights apportionment and adjudication. And incentives established at the basin level for groundwater recharge have been an important tool to facilitate drought resiliency and inter-jurisdictional cooperation in the basin. These same policies, which have proven successful in some inter-state contexts within the United States, are worthy of consideration by international river basin commissions and the international legal community in general.

On the other hand, two centuries of dealing with transboundary water management have produced at least as many missteps as successes in the United States, and learning to avoid those mistakes could be even more helpful to the development and implementation of international water law than attempting to imitate U.S. successes. Arbitrary line-drawing in water policy—whether between raw water and virtual water in commerce or between groundwater and surface water in rights allocation—tends to lead to legal uncertainty and water disputes. Laws and policies based on inaccurate or out-of-date data or models create rigid legal expectations and poor water planning.

More research is needed on the degree to which the successes or failures in transboundary water management in the United States are functions of unique cultural, legal, and geographic conditions in the United States and to what extent they are transferrable in other transboundary contexts internationally. Many of the challenges and opportunities in inter-state water issues are evident in international water management, but inter-state water law has the advantage of avoiding many of the differences in laws and culture more prevalent in the international context, while enjoying the benefit of a unifying and preemptive national power. Ultimately, however, the prescriptions for effective transboundary water management—establishing jurisdiction at the appropriate geographic scope to limit externalities and transaction costs, and integrated management through collaborative, inclusive, and adaptive governance institutions—will serve to more effectively develop and protect transboundary waters at both the sub-national and supranational levels.

List of References

Abbott, Kenneth W., & Duncan Snidal, 'Strengthening International Regulation through Transnational New Governance: Overcoming the Orchestration Deficit,' *Vanderbilt Journal of Transnational Law*, Vol. 42(2) (2009), pp. 501–578.

Abderrahman, Walid A., 'Energy and Water in Arid Developing Countries: Saudi Arabia, A Case-Study,' *International Journal of Water Resources Development*, Vol. 17(2) (2010), pp. 247–255.

Abrams, Robert H., 'Transboundary Water Allocation Risks of Compacts: Who Wins When Legal Rules Face Adaptive Challenges,' *Rocky Mountain Mineral Law Institute*, Vol. 60, c. 9–1 (2014).

Abrams, Robert H., 'Water, Climate Change, and the Law: Integrated Eastern States Water Management Founded on a New Cooperative Federalism,' *Environmental Law Reporter, News & Analysis*, Vol. 42(5) (2012), pp. 10433–10449.

Acordo sobre o Aquífero Guarani [Agreement on the Guarani Aquifer], 2 August 2010, Argentina-Brazil-Paraguay-Uruguay, Ministério Das Relações Exteriores [Brazilian Ministry of Foreign Affairs].

Adler, Robert W., 'Climate Change and the Hegemony of State Water Law,' *Stanford Environmental Law Journal*, Vol. 29(1) (2010), pp. 1–61.

Adler, Robert W., 'The Ancient Mariner of Constitutional Law: The Historical, Yet Declining Role of Navigability,' *Washington University Law Review*, Vol. 90(2) (2013), pp. 1643–1706.

Agreement Between the Government of the Hashemite Kingdom of Jordan and the Government of the Kingdom of Saudi Arabia for the Management and Utilization of the Ground Waters of the Al-Sag/Al-Disi Layer (April 20, 2015), http://www.internationalwaterlaw.org/documents/regionaldocs/Disi_Aquifer_Agreement-English2015.pdf.

Allan, J. A., 'Virtual Water—The Water, Food, and Trade Nexus: Useful Concept or Misleading Metaphor?,' *Water International*, Vol. 28(1) (2003), pp. 106–113.

Allan, J. A., 'Virtual Water—Part of an Invisible Synergy that Ameliorates Water Scarcity,' *in*, Peter Rogers, Ramon Llamas, & Luis Martinez-Cortina (eds.), *Water Crisis: Myth or Reality*, pp. 131–150 (Taylor & Francis, 2006).

Anderson, Terry L., & Clay J. Landry, 'Exporting Water to the World,' *Water Resources Update(Journal of Contemporary Water Research and Education)*, Vol. 118(1), pp. 60–67 (2001).

Arizona Revised Statutes §§ 48–3771–3783 (2017).

Arizona v. California, 373 U.S. 546 (1963).

Arkansas Democrat-Gazette v. Zimmerman, 20 S.W.3d 301, 304.

Arnold, Craig Anthony, 'Adaptive Watershed Planning and Climate Change,' *Environmental & Energy Law & Policy*, Vol. 5(2) (2010), pp. 417–487.

Arnold, Craig Anthony, 'Fourth-Generation Environmental Law: Integrationist and Multimodal,' *William & Mary Environmental Law & Policy Review*, Vol. 35(3) (2011), pp. 771–884.

August, Jack L., Jr., *The Vision in the Desert: Carl Hayden and Hydropolitics in the American Southwest* (Texas Christian University Press, 1999).

Bean v. Morris, 221 U.S. 485, 496–87 (1911).

Biber, Eric, 'The Price of Admission: Causes, Effects, and Patterns of Conditions Imposed on States Entering the Union,' *American Journal of Legal History*, Vol. 46(2) (2004), pp. 119–208.

Blomgren Bingham, Lisa, 'The Next Generation of Administrative Law: Building the Legal Infrastructure for Collaborative Governance,' *Wisconsin Law Review*, Vol. 2010(2) (2010), pp. 297–356.

Blumm, Michael C., & Rachel D. Guthrie, 'Internationalizing the Public Trust Doctrine: Natural Law and Constitutional and Statutory Approaches to Fulfilling the Saxion Vision,' *UC Davis Law Review*, Vol. 45(3) (2012), pp. 741–808.

Boelens, Rutgerd, Armando Guevara-Gil, & Aldo Panfichi, 'Indigenous Water Rights in the Andes: Struggles Over Resources and Legitimacy,' *Journal of Water Law*, Vol. 20(5) (2009), pp. 268–277.

Bonnheim, Noah Byron, 'History of Climate Engineering,' *Climate Change*, Vol. 1(4) (2010), pp. 891–897.

Boulder Canyon Project Act, 45 Stat. 1057 (1928) (codified at 43 U.S.C. § 617–617u (2014)).

Bradshaw, Karen, & Dean Lueck (eds.), *Wildfire Policy: Law and Economics Perspectives* (RFF Press, 2012).

Bradshaw, Karen, & Dean Lueck, 'Contracting for Control of Landscapes,' *Iowa Law Review*, Vol. 100(6) (2015), pp. 2507–2549.

Bretsen, Stephen N., & Peter J. Hill, 'Water Markets as a Tragedy of the Anticommons,' *William & Mary Environmental Law & Policy Review*, Vol. 33(3) (2009), pp. 723–783.

Brown Weiss, Edith, 'The Coming Water Crisis: A Common Concern of Humankind,' *Transnational Environmental Law*, Vol. 1(1) (2012), pp. 153–168.

Brown Weiss, Edith, 'Water Transfers and International Trade Law,' *in*, Edith Brown Weiss, Laurence Boisson de Chazournes & Nathalie Bernasconi-Osterwalder (eds.), *Fresh Water and International Economic Law*, pp. 61–92 (Oxford University Press, 2005).

Bruhl, Aaron-Andrew P., 'Hierarchically Variable Deference to Agency Interpretations,' *Notre Dame Law Review*, Vol. 89(2) (2013), pp. 727–784.

Bureau of Reclamation, Colorado River Interim Guidelines for the Operation of Lower Basin Shortages and Coordinated Operations for Lake Powell and Lake Mead, 73 F.R. 19873–01 (2008).

Campbell, Robert L. & Anthony T. Jones, 'Appropriate Disposal of Effluent from Coastal Desalination Facilities,' *Desalination*, Vol. 182(1) (2005), pp. 365–372.

Cannon, Bill, *Texas: Land of Legend and Lore* (Republic of Texas Press, 2004).

Cappaert v. United States, 426 U.S. 128, 141 (1976).

Carstens, Anne-Marie C., 'Lurking in the Shadows of Judicial Process: Special Masters in the Court's Original Jurisdiction Cases,' *Minnesota Law Review*, Vol. 86(2) (2002), pp. 625–715.

Cazurra, Tomás, 'Water Reuse of South Barcelona's Wastewater Reclamation Plant,' *Desalination*, Vol. 218(1) (2008), pp. 43–51.

Coase, Ronald, 'The Problem of Social Cost,' *Journal of Law & Economics*, Vol. 3(1) (1960), pp. 1–44.

Colorado River Compact, 70 Cong. Rec. 325 (1928).

Colorado v. Kansas, 320 U.S. 383, 392 (1943).

Colorado v. New Mexico, 459 U.S. 176 (1982).

Complaint at 2–7, *Wind River Resources LLC v. Frisby*, No. 2:08-cv-00653-KJD-GWF (D. Nev. May 21, 2008).

Constitution of Ecuador (2008).

Convention on the Law of Non-navigational Uses of International Watercourses, G.A. Res. 51 Res. 51/229, UN GAOR, 51st Sess., Supp. No. 49, UN Doc. A/RES/51/229 (July 8, 1997).

Convention on the Protection, Utilisation, Recharge and Monitoring of the Franco-Swiss Genevois Aquifer (January 1, 2008).

Cooter, Robert D., *The Strategic Constitution* (Princeton University Press, 2000).

Craig, Robin Kundis, "'Stationarity is Dead'—Long Live Transformation: Five Principles for Climate Change Adaptation Law," *Harvard Environmental Law Review*, Vol. 34(1) (2009), pp. 9–73.

Craig, Robin Kundis, 'Comparative Guide to Western States' Public Trust Doctrines: Public Values, Private Rights, and the Evolution Toward an Ecological Public Trust,' *Ecology Law Quarterly*, Vol. 37(1) (2010), pp. 53–197.

Craig, Robin Kundis, 'Constitutional Contours for the Design and Implementation of Multistate Renewable Energy Programs and Projects,' *University of Colorado Law Review*, Vol. 81(3) (2010), pp. 771–832.

Craig, Robin Kundis, 'Hydraulic Fracturing (Fracking), Federalism, and the Water-Energy Nexus,' *Idaho Law Review*, Vol. 49(2) (2013), pp. 242–264.

Culyer v. Adams, 449 U.S. 433, 438 (1981).

Davenport, James H., 'Softening the Divides: The Seven Colorado River Basin States' Recommendation to the Secretary of the Interior Regarding Lower Basin Shortage Guidelines and the Operation of Lakes Mead and Powell in the Low Reservoir Conditions,' *University of Denver Water Law Review*, Vol. 10 (2) (2007), pp. 287–312.

Davis, Seth, 'The False Promise of Fiduciary Government,' *Notre Dame Law Review*, Vol. 89(3) (2014), pp. 1145–1207.

Davis, Seth, 'Tribal Rights of Action,' *Columbia Human Rights Law Review*, Vol. 45(2) (2014), pp. 499–551.

deBuys, William, ed., *Seeing Things Whole: The Essential John Wesley Powell* (Island Press, 2001).

Delaware River Basin Compact, Pub. L. No. 87–328, 75 Stat. 688 (1961), http://www.state.nj.us/drbc/library/documents/compact.pdf.

Dellapenna, Joseph W., 'Interstate Struggles Over Rivers: The Southeastern States and the Struggle Over the *Hooch,' *NYU Environmental Law Journal*, Vol. 12(1) (2005), pp. 828–900.

Dellapenna, Joseph W., 'The Evolution of Riparianism in the United States,' *Marquette Law Review*, Vol. 95(2) (2011), pp. 53–90.

Dennis, Arnett S., 'Weather Modification by Cloud Seeding,' *International Geophysics Series*, Vol. 24(3) (1980).

Eckstein, Gabriel, 'A Hydrogeological Perspective on the Status of Groundwater Resources under the UN Watercourse Convention,' *Columbia Journal of Environmental Law*, Vol. 30(2) (2005), pp. 525–564.

Eckstein, Gabriel, 'Hydraulic Harmony or Water Whimsy? Guarani Aquifer Countries Sign Agreement,' *International Water Law Project Blog* (August 5, 2010), http://www.internationalwaterlaw.org/blog/2010/08/05/hydraulic-harmony-or-water-whimsy-guarani-aquifer-countries-sign-agreement/.

Engel, Kirsten, 'State Environmental Standard-Setting: Is There a 'Race' and is it 'To the Bottom'?,' *Hastings Law Journal*, Vol. 48(3) (1997), pp. 271–398.

Evans, Allison, 'The Groundwater/Surface Water Dilemma in Arizona: A Look Back and a Look Ahead Toward Conjunctive Management Reform,' *Phoenix Law Review*, Vol. 3(1) (2010), pp. 269–292.

Featherstone, Jeffrey P., 'Existing Interstate Compacts: The Law and the Lessons,' *Toledo Journal of Great Lakes Law, Science, and Policy*, Vol. 4(2) (2001), pp. 271–282.

Fleck, John, 'On the Brink of a Major Deal to Reduce Colorado River Water Use,' *Inkstain* (November 6, 2016), http://www.inkstain.net/fleck/2016/11/brink-major-deal-reduce-colorado-river-water-use/.

Fleming, James R., 'The Climate Engineers,' *The Wilson Quarterly*, Vol. 31(2) (2007), pp. 46–60.

Frank, Richard M., 'The Public Trust Doctrine: Assessing its Recent Past and Charting its Future,' *UC Davis Law Review*, Vol. 45(3) (2012), pp. 665–691.

Garner, Eric L., & Michelle Ouellette, 'Future Shock? The Law of the Colorado River in the Twenty-First Century,' *Arizona State Law Journal*, Vol. 27(3) (1995), pp. 469–506.

General Agreement on Tariffs and Trade, October 30, 1947, 61 Stat. A-11, 55 *UNTS* 194.

Getches, David H., 'Indigenous Peoples' Rights to Water Under International Norms,' *Colorado Journal of International Environmental Law & Policy*, Vol. 16(1) (2005), pp. 259–294.

Getches, David H., *Water Law in a Nutshell* 4th ed. (West Academic Publishing, 2009).

Getzler, Joshua, *A History of Water Rights at Common Law* (Oxford University Press, 2004).

Gilligan, Michael J., 'The Transaction Costs Approach to International Institutions, Power, Interdependence and Non-State Actors,' *in*, Helen V. Milner & Andrew

Moravcsik, eds., *Power, Interdependence and Nonstate Actors in World Politics*, pp. 50–65 (Princeton University Press, 2009).

Girardot, Joseph W., 'Toward a Rational Scheme of Inter-state Water Compact Adjudication,' *University of Michigan Journal of Legal Reform*, Vol. 23(1) (1989), pp. 151–177.

Glennon, Robert, & Jacob Kavkewitz, "'A Smashing Victory?' Was *Arizona v. California* a Victory for the State of Arizona?," *Arizona Journal of Environmental Law & Policy*, Vol. 4(1) (2013), pp. 1–38.

Glennon, Robert, & Thomas Maddock, III, 'In Search of Subflow: Arizona's Futile Effort to Separate Groundwater from Surface Water,' *Arizona Law Review*, Vol. 36(2) (1994), pp. 567–607.

Glicksam, Robert L., & Richard E. Levy, 'A Collective Action Perspective on Ceiling Preemption by Federal Environmental Regulation: The Case of Global climate Change,' *Northwestern University Law Review*, Vol. 102(2) (2008), pp. 579–648.

Grant, Douglas L., 'Inter-state Water Allocation Compacts: When the Virtue of Permanence Becomes the Vice of Inflexibility,' *University of Colorado Law Review*, Vol. 74(4) (2003), pp. 105–180.

Hall, Noah D., 'Inter-state Water Compacts and Climate Change Adaptation,' *Environmental & Energy Law & Policy Journal*, Vol. 5(2) (2010), pp. 237–323.

Hall, Noah D., & Benjamin Cavataro, 'Inter-state Groundwater Law in the Snake Valley: Equitable Apportionment and a New Model for Transboundary Aquifer Management,' *Utah Law Review*, Vol. 2013(3) (2013), pp. 1553–1626.

Hardberger, Amy, 'Powering the Tap Dry: Regulatory Alternatives for the Energy-Water Nexus,' *University of Colorado Law Review*, Vol. 84(3) (2013), pp. 529–579.

Hardberger, Amy, 'What Lies Beneath: Determining the Necessity of International Groundwater Policy Along the United States-Mexico Border and a Roadmap to an Agreement,' *Texas Tech Law Review*, Vol. 35(1) (2004), pp. 1211–1258.

Harse, Grant, 'Nebraska's Costs of Compliance with the Republican River Compact: An Equitable Solution,' *Kansas Journal of Law and Public Policy*, Vol. 19(1) (2009), pp. 124–147.

Hasday, Jill Elaine, 'Inter-state Compacts in a Democratic Society: The Problem of Permanency,' *Florida Law Review*, Vol. 49(1) (1997), pp. 1–47.

Hayton, Robert D., & Albert E. Utton, 'Transboundary Groundwaters: The Bellagio Draft Treaty,' *Natural Resources Journal*, Vol. 29(3) (1989), pp. 663–722.

Heller, Michael A., 'The Boundaries of Private Property,' *Yale Law Journal*, Vol. 108(2) (1999), pp. 1163–1223.

Hibbert, Alden R., 'Water Yield Improvement Potential by Vegetation Management on Western Rangelands,' *Journal of American Water Resources Association*, Vol. 19(3) (1983), pp. 375–381.

Hirokawa, Keith, 'Some Pragmatic Observations about Radical Critique in Environmental Law,' *Stanford Environmental Law Journal*, Vol. 21(1) (2002), pp. 225–235.

Hobbs, Gregory J., Jr., 'Eighth Update to Colorado Water Law: An Historical Overview,' *University of Denver Water Law Review*, Vol. 16(1) (2012), 137.

Hobbs, Gregory J., Jr., 'The Role of Climate in Shaping Western Water Institutions,' *University of Denver Water Law Review*, Vol. 7(1) (2003), pp. 1–46.

Hoekstra, Y., & A. K. Chapagain, 'Water Footprints of Nations: Water Use by People as a Function of Their Consumption Pattern,' *Water Resources Management*, Vol. 21(1) (2007), pp, 35–48.

Hudson County Water Co. v. McCarter, 209 U.S. 349 (1908).

Hudson, Blake, 'Reconstituting Land-Use Federalism to Address Transitory and Perpetual Disasters: The Bimodal Federalism Framework,' *BYU Law Review*, Vol. 2011(6) (2011), pp. 1991–2061.

Hughes v. Oklahoma, 441 U.S. 322, 336 (1979).

In re Gen. Adjudication of All Rights to Use Water in Big Horn River System, 753 P.2d 76, 101 (Wyo. 1988).

In re the Gen. Adjudication of All Rights to Use Water in the Gila River System & Source, 35 P.3d 68, 78–80 (Ariz. 2001).

International Law Association, Helsinki Rules on the Uses of the Waters of International Rivers and Comments, Report of the Fifty-Second Conference (1966).

Inter-American Charter of Social Guarantees, 1948, reprinted in *Encyclopedia of the United Nations and International Relations* 763, 1012 (Edmund Jan Osmanczyk ed., 2003).

International Boundary and Water Commission, Minute 319: Interim International Cooperative Measures in the Colorado River Basin through 2017 and Extension of Minute 318 Cooperative Measures to Address the Continued Effects of the April 2010 Earthquake in the Mexicali Valley, Baja California (November 20, 2012).

International Joint Commission, 'Protection of the Waters of the Great Lakes, Final Report 6,' *International Joint Commission* (2000).

International Law Association, 'Final Report of the Water Resources Law Committee, in Report of the Seventy-First Conference of the International Law Association,' *International Law Association* (2004), http://www.ila-hq.org/pdf/Water%20 Resources/Final%20Report%202004.pdf.

Interstate Council on Water Policy, 'Interstate River Basin Organization Source Water Protection Survey,' *Interstate Council on Water Policy* (February 2012), http://www.icwp.org/cms/ic/Inter-stateReport_new.pdf.

Interstate Water Apportionment Compacts, U.S. Fish and Wildlife Service, http://www.fws.gov/laws/lawsdigest/compact.html.

Johnson, Nathan C., 'Protecting Our Water Compacts: The Looming Threat of Unilateral Congressional Interaction,' *Wisconsin Law Review*, Vol. 2010(3) (2010), pp. 875–905.

Kansas v. Colorado, 206 U.S. 46 (1907).

Kansas v. Nebraska, 135 S. Ct. 1042 (2015).

Kemmis, Denial, *This Sovereign Land: A New Vision for Governing the West* (Island Press, 2001).

Khalili, Morteza Sr., et al., 'Results of Cloud Seeding Operations for Precipitation Enhancement in Iran during 1999–2007,' *Planned and Inadvertent Weather Modification/Weather Modification Association* (April 22, 2008), http://ams.confex.com/ams/17WModWMA/techprogram/paper_139149.htm.

Kibel, Paul S., 'Grasp on Water: A Natural Resource that Eludes NAFTA's Notion of Investment,' *Ecology Law Quarterly*, Vol. 34(2) (2007), pp. 655–672.

Kim, Young M., et al., 'Overview of Systems Engineering Approaches for Large-Scale Seawater Desalination Plant with a Reverse Osmosis Network,' *Desalination*, Vol. 238(3) (2009), pp. 312–332.

King, Jonathan S., Peter W. Culp, & Carlos de la Parra, 'Getting to the Right Side of the River: Lessons for Binational Cooperation on the Road to Minute 319,' *University of Denver Water Law Review*, Vol. 18(1) (2014), pp. 35–114.

Kitze, Rachel A., 'Moving Past Preemption: Enhancing the Power of Local Governments Over Hydraulic Fracturing,' *Minnesota Law Review*, Vol. 98(1) (2013), pp. 385–418.

Klein, Christine A., 'The Dormant Commerce Clause and Water Export: Toward a New Analytical Paradigm,' *Harvard Environmental Law Review*, Vol. 35(1) (2011), pp. 131–154.

Klein, Christine A., 'The Environmental Commerce Clause,' *Harvard Environmental Law Review*, Vol. 27(1) (2003), pp. 1–70.

Klein, Christine A., 'Water Bankruptcy,' *Minnesota Law Review*, Vol. 97(2) (2012), pp. 560–624.

Kohloff, Karl, & David Roberts, 'Beyond the Colorado River: Is an International Water Augmentation Consortium in Arizona's Future?,' *Arizona Law Review*, Vol. 49(2) (2007), pp. 257–286.

Kourides, P. Nicholas, 'The Influence of Islamic Law on Contemporary Middle Eastern Legal Systems: The Formation and Binding Force of Contracts,' *Columbia Journal of Transnational Law*, Vol. 9(1) (1970), pp. 384–435.

Kyl, Jon, & Ryan A Smith, 'Forward: Water Law and Policy Conference,' *Arizona Law Review*, Vol. 49(2) (2007), pp. 209–216.

Larson, Rhett B., 'Augmented Water Law,' *Texas Tech Law Review*, Vol. 48(3) (2016), pp. 757–781.

Larson, Rhett B., 'Holy Water and Human Rights: Indigenous Peoples' Religious-Rights Claims to Water Resources,' *Arizona Journal of Environmental Law & Policy*, Vol. 2(1) (2011), pp. 81–109.

Larson, Rhett B., 'Innovation and International Commons: The Case of Desalination under International Law,' *Utah Law Review*, Vol. 2012(2) (2012), pp. 759–819.

Larson, Rhett B., 'Interstitial Federalism,' *UCLA Law Review*, Vol. 62(4) (2015), pp. 908–968.

Larson, Rhett B., 'Reconciling Energy and Food Security,' *University of Richmond Law Review*, Vol. 48(4) (2014), pp, 929–958.

Larson, Rhett B., 'The Case of Canadian Bulk Water Exports,' *Canadian Global Affairs Institute* (2015), https://d3n8a8pro7vhmx.cloudfront.net/cdfai/pages/609/attachments/original/1440452326/Canadian_Bulk_Water_Exports.pdf?1440452326.

Larson, Rhett B., 'The New Right in Water,' *Washington & Lee Law Review*, Vol. 70(4) (2013), pp. 2181–2267.

Larson, Rhett, & Kelly Kennedy, 'Bankrupt Rivers,' *UC Davis Law Review*, Vol. 49(4) (2016), pp. 1335–1383.

Boisson de Chazournes, Laurence, *International Law and Freshwater: The Multiple Challenges* (Edward Elgar, 2013).

Lehigh Falls Fishing Club v. Andrejewski, 123 A.2d 636 (Pa. 1956).

Leib, Ethan J., David L. Ponet & Michael Serota, 'A Fiduciary Theory of Judging,' *California Law Review*, Vol. 101(3) (2013), pp. 699–753.

Leib, Ethan J., David L. Ponet, & Michael Serota, 'Translating Fiduciary Principles into Public Law,' *Harvard Law Review Forum*, Vol. 126(3) (2013), pp. 91–101.

Lincecum, Jerry B., 'Red River Bridge War,' *in*, Kenneth L. Untied (ed.), *Folklore in Motion: Texas Travel Lore*, pp. 25–34 (University of North Texas Press, 2007).

Long, Elisabeth, '*Wyoming v. USDA*: A Look Down the Road at Management of Inventoried Roadless Areas for Climate Change Mitigation and Adaptation,' *Ecology Law Quarterly*, Vol. 40(2) (2013), pp. 329–383.

Loomis, Brandon, 'Reduction in Tree Cover Over Rivers Could Mean More Water Flow,' *The Arizona Republic* (October 30, 2015).

Loucks, Daniel P., 'Managing America's Rivers: Who's Doing It?,' *International Journal of River Basin Management*, Vol. 1(1) (2003), pp. 21–31.

Louisiana v. Mississippi, 516 U.S. 221 (1995).

Lubowski, Ruben, Marlow Vesterby, Shawn Bucholtz, Alba Baez, and Michael J. Roberts, Major Uses of Land in the United States, 2002, EIB-14 (U.S. Department of Agriculture, Economic Research Service, 2006).

MacDonnell, Lawrence J., '*Arizona v. California*: Its Meaning and Significance for the Colorado River and Beyond After Fifty Years,' *Arizona Journal of Environmental law & Policy*, Vol. 4(1) (2013), pp. 88–129.

Maravilla, Christopher S., 'The Canadian Bulk Water Moratorium and its Implications for NAFTA,' *Currents: International Trade Law Journal*, Vol. 10(1) (2001), pp. 29–35.

Martin v. Waddell's Lessee, 41 U.S. 367, 411 (1842).

Matson, Jeffrey T., 'Interstate Water Compact Version 3.0: Missouri River Basin Compact Drafters Should Consider an Inter-Sovereign Approach to Accommodate Federal and Tribal Interests in Water Resources,' *North Dakota Law Review*, Vol. 88(1) (2012), pp. 97–138.

Mayland, Kirt, 'Navigating the Murky Waters of Connecticut's Water Allocation Scheme,' *Quinnipiac Law Review*, Vol. 24(2), 885 (2006).

McCaffrey, Stephen C., 'The International Law Commission Adopts Draft Articles on International Watercourses,' *American Journal of International Law*, Vol. 89(2) (1995), pp. 395–404.

McConkey, Diane E., 'Federal Reserved Rights to Instream Flows in the National Forests,' *Virginia Environmental Law Journal*, Vol. 13(2) (1994), pp. 305–322.

McCormick, Zachary L., 'Interstate Water Allocation Compacts in the Western United States—Some Suggestions,' *Water Resources Bulletin*, Vol. 30(3) (1994), pp. 385–395.

Missouri v. Illinois, 200 U.S. 496, 521 (1906).

Montana v. Wyoming, 131 S.Ct. 1765 (2011).

Morrison, Michael D., & Keith Dollahite, 'The Public Trust Doctrine: Insuring the Needs of Texas Bays and Estuaries,' *Baylor Law Review*, Vol. 37(3) (1985), pp. 365–424.

Naff, Thomas, 'Islamic Law and the Politics of Water,' *in*, Joseph W. Dellapenna & Joyeeta Gupta (eds.), *The Evolution of the Law and Politics of Water*, pp. 37–52 (Springer, 2008).

Naff, Thomas, & Joseph Dellapenna, 'Can There Be a Confluence? A Comparative Consideration of Western and Islamic Fresh Water Law,' *Water Policy*, Vol. 4(6) (2002), pp. 465–489.

National Park & Conservation Association v. Stanton, 54 F. Supp. 2d 7 (D.D.C. 1999).

Nebraska Revise Statutes § 46–613.01 (2015).

Nebraska v. Iowa, 143 U.S. 359 (1892).

Nebraska v. Wyoming, 325 U.S. 589 (1945).

Nebraska v. Wyoming, 515 U.S. 1115 (1995).

North American Free Trade Agreement, December 8, 1993, 107 Stat. 2057, 32 I.L.M. 289.

O'Leary, Marilyn C., 'The Bellagio Draft Treaty as a Tool for Solving Border Groundwater Issues,' U.S.-*Mexico Law Journal*, Vol. 11(1) (2003), pp. 57–60.

Pahl-Wostl, Claudia, 'Transitions Towards Adaptive Management of Water Facing Climate and Global Change,' *Water Resource Management*, Vol. 21(1) (2007), pp. 49–62.

Parlow, Matthew J., 'Civic Republicanism, Public Choice Theory, and Neighborhood Councils: A New Model for Civic Engagement,' *University of Colorado Law Review*, Vol. 79(3) (2008), pp. 137–188.

Paschal Osborn, Rachael, 'Climate Change and the Columbia River Treaty,' *Washington Journal of Environmental Law & Policy*, Vol. 2(1) (2012), pp. 75–123.

Patashnik, Josh, '*Arizona v. California* and the Equitable Apportionment of Interstate Waterways,' *Arizona Law Review*, Vol. 56(1) (2014), pp. 1–51.

Pedraza-Fariña, Laura , 'Conceptions of Civil Society in International Lawmaking and Implementation: A Theoretical Framework,' *Michigan Journal of International Law*, Vol. 34(3) (2013), pp. 605–673.

Pike v. Bruce Church, 397 U.S. 137, 142 (1970).

Pollard's Lessee v. Hagen, 44 U.S. 212, 216 (1845).

PPL Montana, LLC v. Montana, 132 S. Ct. 1215, 1235 (2012).

Price, Dean Waters, 'The Legal and Historical Barriers to Out-of-District Transfers from Mainstream Colorado River Irrigation Districts in Arizona,' *University of Denver Water Law Review*, Vol. 15(1) (2011), pp. 5–29.

Programme for the Development of a Regional Strategy for the Utilisation of the Nubian Sandstone Aquifer System—Terms of Reference for the Monitoring and Exchange of Groundwater Information of the Nubian Sandstone Aquifer System (Tripoli, October 5, 2000).

Rauscher, H. Michael, 'Ecosystem Management Decision Support for Federal Forests in the United States: A Review,' *Forest Ecology and Management*, Vol. 114(2–3) (1999), pp. 173–197.

Red River Compact Act of December 22, 1980, Pub. L. No. 96–564, 94 Stat. 3305.

Reeder, Laura, 'Creating a Legal Framework for Regulation of Natural Gas Extraction from the Marcellus Shale Formation,' *William & Mary Environmental Law & Policy Review*, Vol. 34(3) (2010), pp. 999–1026.

Reiblich, Jesse, & Christine A. Klein, 'Climate Change and Water Transfers,' *Pepperdine Law Review*, Vol. 41(3) (2014), pp. 439–508.

Reisner, Marc, *Cadillac Desert: The American West and Its Disappearing Water* (Penguin Books, 1993).

Republican River Compact, Kan. Stat. Ann. §82a–518 (1942).

Rose, Carol, 'The Comedy of the Commons: Custom, Commerce, and Inherently Public Property,' *University of Chicago Law Review*, Vol. 53(3) (1986), pp. 711–781.

Rosenbloom, Jonathan, 'New Day at the Pool: State Preemption, Common Pool Resources, and Non-Place Based Municipal Collaborations,' *Harvard Environmental Law Review*, Vol. 36(2) (2012), pp. 445–485.

Rowberry, Ryan, 'Drinking from the Same Cup: Federal Reserved Water Rights and National Parks in the Eastern United States,' *Georgia State University Law Review*, Vol. 29(4) (2013), pp. 987–1023.

Ruhl, J. B., 'General Design Principles for Resilience and Adaptive Capacity in Legal Systems—With Application to Climate Change Adaptation,' *North Carolina Law Review*, Vol. 89(5) (2011), pp. 1373–1403.

Ryan, Erin, 'Negotiating Federalism,' *Boston College Law Review*, Vol. 52(1) (2011), pp. 1–136.

Sadoff, Claudia W., & David Grey, 'Beyond the River: The Benefits of Cooperation on International Rivers,' *Water Policy*, Vol. 4(5) (2002), pp. 389–403.

Salman, Salman, 'The Helsinki Rules, the UN Watercourses Convention and the Berlin Rules: Perspectives on International Law,' *Water Resources Development*, Vol. 23(4) (2007), pp. 625–640.

Salman, Salman, 'Inter-States Water Disputes in India: An Analysis of the Settlement Process,' *Water Policy*, Vol. 4(3) (2002), pp. 223–237.

Sarine, L. Elizabeth, 'The Supreme Court's Problematic Deference to Special Masters in Interstate Water Disputes,' *Ecology Law Quarterly*, Vol. 39(2) (2012), pp. 535–569.

Sax, Joseph L., 'The Limits of Private Rights in Public Waters,' *Environmental Law*, Vol. 19(2) (1989), pp. 473–483.

Sax, Joseph L., 'The Public Trust Doctrine in Natural Resource Law: Effective Judicial Intervention,' *Michigan Law Review*, Vol. 68(1) (1970), pp. 471–566.

Sax, Joseph L., et al. *Legal Control of Water Resources, Cases and Materials* 4th ed. (Thomson West, 2006).

Saxer, Shelley Ross, 'The Fluid Nature of Property Rights in Water,' *Duke Environmental Law & Policy Forum*, Vol. 21(1) (2010), pp. 49–112.

Schäferhoff, Marco et al., 'Transnational Public-Private Partnerships in International Relations: Making Sense of Concepts, Research Frameworks, and Results,' *International Studies Review*, Vol. 11(3) (2009), pp. 451–474.

Shively v. Bowlby, 152 U.S. 1 (1894).

Smit, Erica C., 'Geoengineering: Issues of Accountability in International Law,' *Nevada Law Journal*, Vol. 15(2) (2015), pp. 1060–1089.

South Carolina v. North Carolina, 130 S. Ct. 854 (2010).

Sporhase v. Nebraska, 458 U.S. 941 (1982).

Squillace, Mark, & Alexander Hood, 'NEPA, Climate Change, and Public Lands Decision-Making,' *Environmental Law*, Vol. 42(2) (2012), pp. 469–526.

Stanford, J. A., & J. V. Ward, 'Management of Aquatic Resources in Large Catchments: Recognizing Interactions between Ecosystem Connectivity and Environmental Disturbance,' *in*, Robert J. Naiman (ed.), *Watershed Management: Balancing Sustainability and Environmental Change*, pp. 91–124(Springer, 2002).

Stegner, Wallace, *Beyond the Hundredth Meridian: John Wesley Powell and the Second Opening of the West* (Penguin Books, 1954).

Stoa, Ryan B., 'The United Nations Watercourses Convention on the Dawn of Entry Into Force,' *Vanderbilt Journal of Transnational Law*, Vol. 47(5) (2014), pp. 1321–1370.

Strifling, David A., 'An Ecosystem Based Approach to Slowing the Synergistic Effects of Invasive Species and Climate Change,' *Duke Environmental Law & Policy Forum*, Vol. 22(1) (2011), pp. 145–193.

Tarlock, A. Dan, 'The Creation of New Risk Sharing Water Entitlement Regimes: The Case of the Truckee-Carson Settlement,' *Ecology Law Quarterly*, Vol. 25(4) (1999), pp. 674–691.

Tarlock, A. Dan, 'The Law of Equitable Apportionment Revisited, Updated, and Restated,' *University of Colorado Law Review*, Vol. 56(4) (1985), pp. 381–411.

Tarlock, A. Dan, 'The Potential Role of Local Governments in Watershed Management,' *Pace Environmental Law Review*, Vol. 20(1) (2002), pp. 149–176.

Tarlock, A. Dan, 'Towards a More Robust International Water Law of Cooperation to Address Droughts and Ecosystem Conservation,' *Georgetown Environmental Law Review*, Vol. 28(2) (2016), pp. 261–290.

Tarlock, A. Dan, Safeguarding International River Ecosystems in Times of Scarcity, *University of Denver Water Law Review*, Vol. 3(1) (2000), pp. 231–272.

Tarlock, A. Dan, *Law of Water Rights and Resource* (Thomson Reuters, 2000).

Tarlock, A. Dan, & Patricia Wouters, 'Are Shared Benefits of International Waters an Equitable Apportionment?,' *Colorado Journal of International Environmental Law & Policy*, Vol. 18(1) (2007), pp. 523–536.

Tarrant Regional Water District v. Herrmann, 133 S. Ct. 2120 (2013).

Taylor, Holly, 'Tarrant Regional Water District v. Herrmann: Interpreting Silence in Inter-state Water Compacts with Respect to State Boundaries and the Right to Access Water,' *University of Denver Water Law Review*, Vol. 17(1) (2013), pp. 138–155.

Teclaff, Ludwik A., 'Evolution of the River Basin Concept in National and International Water Law,' *Natural Resources Journal*, Vol. 36(2) (1996), pp. 359–391.

Teclaff, Ludwik A., 'The River Basin Concept and Global Climate Change,' *Pace Environmental Law Review*, Vol. 8(2) (1991), pp. 355–388.

Tellinghuisen, Stacy, 'Water for Power Generation: What's the Value?,' *Natural Resources Journal*, Vol. 50(3) (2010), pp. 683–720.

Texas v. New Mexico, 482 U.S. 124, 128 (1987).

Charter of Waters of the Senegal River, 2002, http://iea.uoregon.edu/pages/view_treaty.php?t=2002-SenegalRiverWaterCharter.EN.txt&par=view_treaty_html [http://perma.cc/6C3R-4KWU].

The Daniel Ball, 77 U.S. 557 (1871).

Thompson, Barton H., Jr., 'A Federal Act to Promote Integrated Water Management: Is the CZMA a Useful Model?,' *Environmental Law*, Vol. 42(1) (2012), pp. 201–240.

Thompson, Barton H., Jr., 'The Public Trust Doctrine: A Conservative Reconstruction & Defense,' *Southeastern Environmental Law Journal*, Vol. 15(1) (2006), pp. 47–70.

Tir, Jaroslav, & Douglas M. Stinnett, 'The Institutional Design of Riparian Treaties: The Role of River Issues,' *Journal of Conflict Resolution* , Vol. 55(4) (2011), pp. 606–631.

Treaty Between Canada and the United States of American Relating to Cooperative Development of the Water Resources of the Columbia River Basin, January 17, 1961, 542 *UNTS* 244 (1964).

Treaty Between the United States of America and Mexico Respecting the Utilization of the Colorado and Tijuana Rivers and of the Rio Grande, February 3, 1944, 59 Stat. 1219.

Trelease, Frank J., 'State Water and State Lines: Commerce in Water Resources,' *University of Colorado Law Review*, Vol. 56(4) (1985), pp. 347–379.

Troendle, Charles, Marc Wilcox, Greg Bevenger, & Laurie Porth, 'The Coon Creek Water Yield Augmentation Project: Implementation of Timber Harvesting Technology to Increase Streamflow,' *Forest Ecology and Management*, Vol. 143(1–3) (2001), pp. 179–187.

Truckee-Carson-Pyramid Lake Water Rights Settlement Act, Pub.L. No. 101–618, 104 Stat. 3294 (1990).

United Haulers Association, Inc. v. Oneida-Herkimer Solid Waste Management Authority, 550 U.S. 330, 338 (2007).

United Nations Conference on Environment and Development, Agenda 21, UN Doc. A/CONF.151/26 (Vol. II) (1992).

United Nations Declaration on the Rights of Indigenous Peoples, G.A. Res. 61/295, UN Doc. A/RES61/295 (September 13, 2007).

United State Constitution.

[See Lubowski above] *United States v. Adair*, 723 F.2d 1394, 1414 (9th Cir. 1983).

United States v. New Mexico, 438 U.S. 696, 718 (1978).

Urbina, Ian, 'Drilling Down: Regulation Lax as Gas Wells' Tainted Water Hits River,' *New York Times* (February 26, 2011), http://www.bctwa.org/FrkBC-DrillingDown-NewYorkTimes.pdf.

Vick, Margaret J., 'The Law of International Waters: Reasonable Utilization,' *Chicago-Kent Journal of International & Comparative Law*, Vol. 12(1) (2012), pp. 141–178.

Ware, Eugene F., *Roman Water Law: Translated from the Pendects of Justinian* (West Publishing, 1905).

Watters, Molly M., 'Fish and Federalism: How the Asian Carp Litigation Highlights a Deficiency in the Federal Common Law Displacement Analysis,' *Michigan Journal of Environmental & Administrative Law*, Vol. 2(2) (2013), pp. 535–562.

Weber, Robert F., 'New Governance, Financial Regulation, and Challenges to Legitimacy: The Example of Internal Models Approach to Capital Adequacy Regulation,' *Administrative Law Review*, Vol. 62(3) (2010), pp. 783–869.

Wesley Powell, John, *Report on the Lands of the Arid Region of the United States, with a More Detailed Account of the Lands of Utah* (Harvard Common Press, 1983).

Wesley Powell, John, *The Exploration of the Colorado River and Its Canyons* (Dover Publications Inc., 1961).

West, Chad A., 'For Body, Soul, or Wealth: The Distinction, Evolution, and Policy Implications of a Water Ethic,' *Stanford Environmental Law Journal*, Vol. 26(1) (2007), pp. 201–234.

Wiener, Jonathan B. Wiener, 'Global Environmental Regulation: Instrument Choice in Legal Context,' *Yale Law Journal*, Vol. 108(2) (1999), pp. 677–800.

Williams, B. K., R. C. Szaro & C. D. Shapiro, 'Adaptive Management: The U.S. Department of the Interior Technical Guide,' *Adaptive Management Working Group, U.S. Department of the Interior* (2009), https://www2.usgs.gov/sdc/doc/DOI-%20Adaptive%20ManagementTechGuide.pdf.

Winters v. United States, 207 U.S. 564 (1908).

Woodhouse, Melvin, 'Is Public Participation a Rule of the Law of International Watercourses?,' *Natural Resources Journal*, Vol. 43(1) (2003), pp. 137–183.

World Water Council, 'E-Conference Synthesis: Virtual Water Trade—Conscious Choices,' *World Water Council* (2004), http://www.waterfootprint.org/Reports/virtual_ water_final_synthesis.pdf.

Worster, Donald, *A River Running West: The Life of John Wesley Powell* (Oxford University Press, 2001).

Wyoming v. Colorado, 259 U.S. 419 (1922).

Wyoming v. United States, 492 U.S. 406 (1989).

El-Sayed, Y. M., 'The Rising Potential of Competitive Solar Desalination,' *Desalination*, Vol. 216(1–3) (2007), pp. 314–324.

Young, Ernest A., 'The Rehnquist Court's Two Federalisms,' *Texas Law Review*, Vol. 83(1) (2004), pp. 1–165.

Younos, Tamim, 'Environmental Issues of Desalination,' *Journal of Contemporary Water Research & Education*, Vol. 132(1) (2005), pp. 11–18.

Zellmer, Sandra, 'The Anti-Speculation Doctrine and its Implications for Collaborative Water Management,' *Nevada Law Journal*, Vol. 8(3) (2008), pp. 994–1030.

www.ingramcontent.com/pod-product-compliance
Lightning Source LLC
Chambersburg PA
CBHW031332230926
51848CB00001B/203
9789004357631